Microsoft®
Word 2010 Plain & Simple

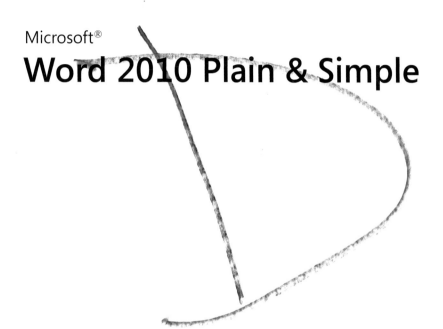

Katherine Murray

PUBLISHED WITH THE AUTHORIZATION OF MICROSOFT CORPORATION BY:
O'Reilly Media, Inc.
1005 Gravenstein Highway North
Sebastopol, California 95472

Printed and bound in Canada.

1 2 3 4 5 6 7 8 9 WCT 5 4 3 2 1 0

Microsoft Press titles may be purchased for educational, business, or sales promotional use. Online editions are also available for most titles (*http://my.safaribooksonline.com*). For more information, contact our corporate/institutional sales department: (800) 998-9938 or *corporate@oreilly.com*. Visit our website at *microsoftpress.oreilly.com*. Send comments to *mspinput@microsoft.com*.

Acquisitions and Developmental Editor: Kenyon Brown
Production Editor: Adam Zaremba
Copy Editor: Nancy Sixsmith
Editorial Production: Octal Publishing, Inc.
Technical Reviewer: Kristen Tod
Compositor: Ron Bilodeau
Illustrator: Robert Romano
Indexer: Ron Strauss

978-0-735-62731-4

To the creative spirit in all of us

Contents

1 About This Book   1

2 Getting Started with Word 2010   7

3 Editing Your Content 29

4 Formatting Documents 59

5 Designing Great Layouts 97

6

Adding Graphics to Your Documents 127

7

Word 2010 for Blogging, Mailing, and More 155

8 Adding Special Features for Long Documents 175

9 Sharing, Co-Authoring, and Finalizing Your Document 195

10

Customizing and Securing Word

What do you think of this book? We want to hear from you!

Microsoft is interested in hearing your feedback so we can continually improve our books and learning resources for you. To participate in a brief online survey, please visit:

www.microsoft.com/learning/booksurvey/

Acknowledgments

Each book is a collaborative process that requires the time, talent, and energy of a number of different people. Thanks to all who contributed to the writing, editing, and layout of this book! Most notably, thanks go out to:

- Marianne Moon and Jerry Joyce, for providing the great starting point for this revision

- Juliana Aldous, at Microsoft Press, for giving me the great opportunity to work on this project

- Claudette Moore, of Moore Literary Agency, for her always-wise counsel and project companionship

- Kenyon Brown, at O'Reilly Media, for his effective management of the many pieces of this book as it went through editorial and production

- Nancy Sixsmith, for an excellent copyedit completed in nearly record time (and with a smile)

- Ron Bilodeau, Rob Romano, Adam Zaremba, and crew, for producing the great layout of the book you now hold in your hands

1

About This Book

Microsoft Word 2010 is a big program with features that can help you produce all kinds of great documents—from simple invitations to sophisticated scientific papers. If you want to get the most from Word 2010 in the shortest amount of time and least amount of effort—and who doesn't?—this book is for you. You'll find *Microsoft® Word 2010 Plain & Simple* to be a straightforward, easy-to-read guide that presents all the how-to's in a clear, visual way. Your computer should help you easily accomplish what you want to do, not require that you work harder or longer, so the purpose of this book is to help you get your work done quickly and efficiently and then push back from the computer and go do the things you really want to do in your life.

No Computerspeak!

Let's face it—when you're trying to finish a task you don't know how to do but you need to get it done in a hurry, or when you're stuck in the middle of a process and can't figure out what to do next, there's nothing more frustrating than having to read page after page of technical background material as you try to find the answers you need. You want only the information you you're looking for—nothing more, nothing less—and you want it now! *Solutions* should be easy to find and understand.

That's what this book is about. It's written in plain English—no technical jargon and no computerspeak. No single task in the book takes more a few pages. And the tasks are presented to you in a simple visual format so that you can lay the book open on your desk and refer to the illustrations as you go. Just look up a task in the index or the table of contents, turn to the page, and there's the information you need, laid out in an illustrated step-by-step format. You don't get bogged down by the whys and wherefores: just follow the steps and get your work done with a minimum of hassle. Occasionally you might have to turn to another page if the procedure you're working on is accompanied by a *See Also*. That's because there's some overlap among tasks, and seeing how they connect can help you learn more about the features. Some useful *Tips* are also scattered here and there in the book, and you'll also find a *Try This* or a *Caution* once in a while. By and large, however, the tasks you'll find here remain true to the heart and soul of the book, which is that the information you need should be available to you at a glance and it should be *plain and simple!*

Useful Tasks...

Whether you use Word 2010 for work, school, personal correspondence, or all of the above, you'll find information on tasks that you perform in all those settings. In this way, what you learn here will relate directly to the work you really need to do in Word.

...And the Easiest Way to Do Them

You'll also find that even when there are several ways to get to the same destination, this book offers the easiest way to accomplish a task. Word often provides a multitude of methods for achieving a single end result—and that flexibility can be daunting or delightful, depending on the way you like to work. If you tend to stick with one favorite and familiar approach, I think the methods described in this book are the way to go. If you like trying out alternative techniques, go ahead! Word 2010 invites exploration, and you may discover ways of doing things that you think are easier or that you like better than the ones shown here. If you do, that's great! It's exactly what the developers of Word 2010 had in mind when they provided so many alternatives.

A Quick Overview

First, this book assumes that Word 2010 is already installed on your computer as a part of a Microsoft Office 2010 suite. If you haven't installed the software yet, don't worry—just insert the first program DVD in the drive, and Windows will prompt you through the rest of the process. So, unlike many computer books, this one doesn't start with installation instructions and a list of system requirements. If Word 2010 is installed on its own without the other Office 2010 applications, you can still use everything in this book except the instructions for those tasks that incorporate material from other Office components.

Next, you don't have to read this book in any particular order. It's designed so that you can jump in, get the information you need, and then close the book and keep it near your computer until the next time you need it. But that doesn't mean the information is scattered with wild abandon. The tasks you want to accomplish are arranged in two levels. The overall type of task you're looking for is under a main heading such as "Creating a New Document" or "Laying Out the Page." Then, in each section of the book, the smaller tasks within each main task are arranged in a loose progression from the simplest to the more complex.

In the overall scheme of the book, this section (Section 1) introduces you to where you're going, giving you an overall game-plan of what's head.

Section 2 covers the basic tasks—and a few slightly more complex ones—that you can use to produce professional-looking documents: starting, saving, reopening, and closing a Word document; entering, editing, formatting, copying, and moving text; working with documents that were created in an earlier version of Word; using Word's research tools; translating foreign-language text; learning how to use the spelling- and grammar-checking tools; and getting some help if you need it. You'll also find out how to use Backstage view to manage your documents and print using the new combined print-and-preview window.

Section 3 takes you beyond the basics and focuses on editing the content you create in Word. You'll find out how to convert old documents to Word 2010; view your document in different ways; use the Navigation Pane to move through the document; research and translate text, and locate items in your file. You'll also find tasks for all the old standby commands no word processing program can do without: copying and pasting, finding and replacing, running the spelling checker, and adding page numbers to your files.

Section 4 is all about formatting your Word documents. You'll discover tasks for designing and formatting your documents, using themes, styles, and fonts to create letters, memos, and other types of frequently used documents. You'll see how simple it is to use Word's Quick Styles feature to create your own styles: custom-formatting text, paragraphs, or an entire document; choosing a theme or creating your own theme to produce documents with consistent design elements; adding decorative touches such as borders and shading; and creating and formatting lists and tables. You also learn about some of the refinements you can apply to your text, such as using the new typography features, *kerning*—that is, adjusting the spacing between characters—and adjusting line spacing in and between paragraphs.

Section 5 is about laying out the page, whether you're creating a simple one-page report or a long document or book whose pages will be printed on both sides and eventually bound. You walk through the steps that are entailed in creating a layout: setting up the margins, flowing text into columns, creating chapters, and fine-tuning the finished document before you print it, including *breaking lines* and eliminating those sad-sounding and unsightly *widows* and *orphans*. You also spend some time in this section discussing tables—creating and customizing them—and you'll learn how useful a table can be in certain layouts.

Section 6 focuses on enhancing your documents with pictures, clip art, drawings, diagrams, charts, and more. You'll learn how to insert a picture into a document; edit, recolor, or resize the picture; use Word 2010's artistic effects to add special touches to images and work with the improved Crop tool to get just the effect you want; add a border or special effects to it—soft edges, glow, 3-D formats, and so on—or wrap text around it; and turn ordinary text into eye-popping art with WordArt. You also learn to create and format diagrams and charts that can bring your dry statistics to life and make them not only more friendly to the eye but more understandable than plain old worksheets and endless columns and rows of numbers.

Section 7 offers tasks on completing specific special tasks in Word, including putting together a mail merge campaign, designing forms, composing blog entries, and much more. These special tasks aren't as daunting as you might think, and this book will help you sail smoothly through the process, from setting up your master document and *data source* to printing your envelopes or mailing labels.

Section 8 specializes in the tasks that you'll need to accomplish if you're putting together a long document. For example, a 50-page report requires things like running heads, a table of contents, and may involve master documents and subdocuments. This section explores these features and also shows you how to set up footnotes and endnotes, and create a table of contents and an index to help your readers find just the information they're looking for in your document.

Section 9 is all about co-authoring in Word 2010. This exciting new feature enables you to edit a document simultaneously with others who are working on the same document. This section introduces you to Windows Live SkyDrive and shows you how to post your files online where you can access them and share them with others. This chapter also shows you the ins and outs of reviewing the documents you share by using tracked changes, adding comments, comparing, and merging the documents you prepare.

Section 10 is about customizing Word 2010 to work the way you do and protecting the files you create. You can take control of just about every aspect of Word—adding items to the Quick Access toolbar, customizing the ribbon and the status bar and color scheme, showing or minimizing the ribbon, creating your own macros, customizing the way Word checks for spelling and grammar errors, and much more. You'll also learn how you can set permissions for your document, work in Protected View, and check the security and readiness of your files before you share them with others.

What's New in Word 2010?

Word 2010 is the newest version of a great word processing program that has been around for a long, long time. The previous version of Word—Word 2007—marked a dramatic shift in the way the program was designed and a big shift in the way people used it. Instead of navigating through a maze of menus, toolbars, and nested dialog boxes (which was part of Word prior to the 2007 version), in Word 2007 a new user interface was introduced in which the ribbon offered all the tools users needed relative to the task at hand. Word 2010 builds on this simplicity of design and efficiency of use idea by presenting users with easy-to-navigate tabs; context-based options; and the ribbon, which you can now customize to include all your favorite tools, new tabs, and even macros that you create.

Another new focus in Word 2010 is on the quality and creativity of the work you produce. Now Word 2010 helps you bring your ideas to life by offering better picture editing tools (an enhanced Crop feature, exciting new artistic effects, and a great Paste with Live Preview tool). You can add special effects to text (glow, shadow, and more) with a click of the mouse; you can create new SmartArt designs; you can take advantage of high-end typography features with one of your favorite OpenType fonts.

And because the world of work is changing quickly and dramatically to include the entire *world* of work, Word 2010 includes dramatic improvements in the features that help you work collaboratively with peers down the hall or around the globe. Co-authoring is a hot new feature in Word 2010 if you're using SharePoint Workspaces 2010 or Windows Live, enabling you to view and contact other authors who are working in your file at the same time you are. New security measures make document protection easier (and actually more invisible) than ever; and great translation tools give you an expanded ability to translate words and phrases—or sections and documents—without leaving the document you're working on.

Finally, the other big story in Word 2010 is the *work anywhere* theme. Nobody is too surprised to learn that the Web is everywhere, and now Word 2010 is everywhere as well. You can easily use the Office Web Apps for Word to save, share, access, and continue your work on important documents whether you're in the office or out in the world. You can keep working on your Word documents from any place you have Web access.

This is just the tip of the iceberg as far as new features go in Word 2010, but rest assured that whether you're creating documents for home, school, or business, there are features in the new release that will help you look better, collaborate more effectively, and work with more flexibility than ever before. Nice.

A Few Assumptions

In order to come up with the kind of content that will be helpful to you, I had to make a few educated guesses about you as I started writing this book. Perhaps your computer is solely for personal use—e-mail, the Internet, and so on. Or you might run a small business or work for a giant corporation. After taking these quite varied possibilities into account, I assumed that you're familiar with computer basics—the keyboard and your little friend the mouse, for example—and that you're connected to the Internet and/or a company intranet. I also assumed that if you're working on a corporate network, you're familiar with the specialized and customized tools, such as a SharePoint site or a file-management system, that are used on the network. I figured you're using either Windows 7 or Windows Vista and that you're pretty familiar with the basic tasks required to open and save files.

Word 2010 has an inviting visual appearance, and it changes depending on what you've selected in your document and the resolution of your screen display. That is, with a high resolution, you'll see many more individual items on the ribbon than you will if you're using a low resolution. With a low resolution, you'll find that items are contained under a button, and only when you click the button are the items then displayed. To see this effect, resize the width of your Word window, and note that items are hidden when you make the window smaller and that they appear when you make the window larger. A screen resolution of 1024 by 768 pixels was used to capture the images in this book so that I could show the best quality images, but this might not be the resolution you use on your own monitor, so the screenshots might look slightly different from the display you see on the screen.

See Also

Whichever version of Windows you're using, you may want to consult two helpful books written by Marianne Moon and Jerry Joyce: *Windows Vista™ Plain & Simple* and *Windows 7 Plain & Simple*. If you want to learn more about the other Office 2010 programs as well, you may want to read *Microsoft® Office 2010 Plain & Simple* (written by yours truly).

A Final Word (or Two)

So are you ready to dive in and begin learning about Word 2010? Just a few more thoughts before you get started.

I have three primary goals for this book:

- I want this book to help you complete your work easily.

- I hope it will introduce you to cool techniques you didn't know about.

- I hope you have as much fun reading and using *Microsoft® Word 2010 Plain & Simple* as I had writing it.

The best way to learn any new task is to dive in and do it (with the proper supports in place, of course). I hope this book provides you with just the support you need to get creative, be productive, and accomplish what you hope to get done with Word 2010.

Getting Started with Word 2010

So what kind of document are you in the mood to create? Microsoft Word 2010 makes it easy for you to design, print, and share professional-looking letters, reports, newsletters, postcards—almost any document you can imagine, you can produce in Word 2010. The screen is organized so that you can find everything easily; the ribbon offers just the tools you need as you work with different objects on your page.

This section gives you a whirlwind tour around the Word 2010 window and introduces you to the basic skills you'll need as you create your content. You discover how to navigate the Word 2010 ribbon and add text, view your document, find what you're looking for, translate phrases and sections, and print what you create.

What's Where in Word?

The Word 2010 window is simple to navigate and easy to use. All the tools you need are within reach, and the program offers a number of views you can use to get different perspectives on the document you're creating. When you first start the program, your document window appears in Print Layout view. Exploring the Word window takes only a few clicks of the mouse. The following two screens give you a sense of the common elements you are likely to see often and show you the different views you can use as you work.

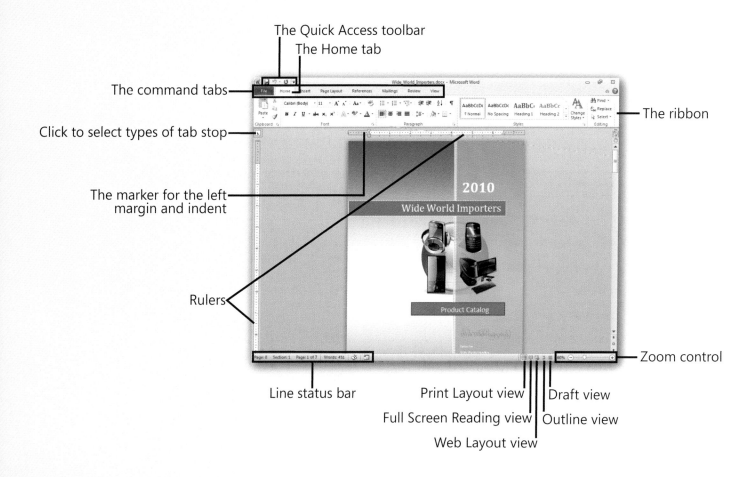

The Quick Access toolbar

The Home tab

The command tabs

The ribbon

Click to select types of tab stop

The marker for the left margin and indent

Rulers

2010

Wide World Importers

Product Catalog

Zoom control

Line status bar

Print Layout view

Draft view

Full Screen Reading view

Outline view

Web Layout view

To help keep the screen uncluttered and the tools easy to find and use, Word brings you just the tools you need when you need them. For example, when you click a picture in your document, the Picture Tools contextual tab appears. Likewise, reviewing tools are available only when you are working with a document that includes tracked changes.

A gallery   Contextual tab   Help

The markup area

Text wrapped around a picture

A paragraph mark

The page number

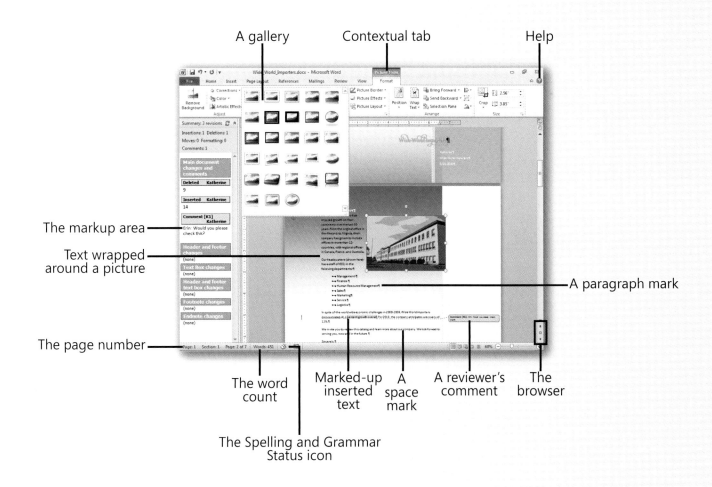

The word count

Marked-up inserted text

A space mark

A reviewer's comment

The browser

The Spelling and Grammar Status icon

Checking Out Word Views

Word 2010 gives you a number of different views you can use as you work with your document in different ways. By default, Print Layout view appears when you start Word; in this view you see the page as it will appear when you print it. Other views make it easy for you to see how your content will look online, review the outline of your document, or display your document in a quick reading view that enables you to scan the text quickly.

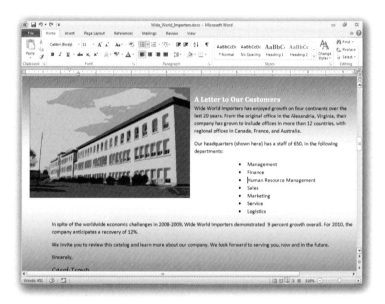

Full Screen Reading view enables you to review a document in a maximized window so that you can do more reading and less scrolling. In Full Screen Reading view, you can add comments, highlight content, translate phrases, and more. You cannot do any editing in this view, however.

Web Layout view makes it easy for you to see how your document will look formatted as a Web page. The big difference between this view and Print Layout view is that you will not see the divisions between the individual pages in your document.

Outline view enables you to see how your document looks when it is displayed according to the various outline levels you've established for your text. You can choose whether to display the text formats—for example, displaying headings in the font size and style they have in the document—or choosing to display text only. You can also move text up and down levels in the outline while you work in Outline view.

Draft view removes a lot of the bells and whistles in the display in Print Layout view and enables you to focus on only your text and pictures. In Draft view you don't see the page divisions that are present in Print Layout view, but you can see pictures, revision marks, tables, and diagrams you create.

Creating a New Document

Launching Word requires just a couple of clicks of the mouse. The Word window opens with a new blank document, ready for your content. If you've been experimenting and Word is already running, you can open a new blank document with a few mouse clicks.

Start Word and Enter Some Text

1. Click the Start button and click All Programs.

2. Click Microsoft Office, and click Microsoft Word 2010.

(continued on next page)

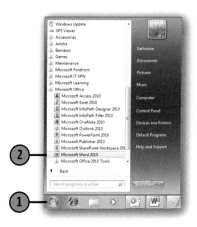

Want to enter some sample text quickly so that you have something to work with? Just type **=rand()** at the point in the document where you want to add sample paragraphs, and Word does the rest. If you want to insert sample Latin text, use **=lorem()** instead.

To better see the formatting marks as well as your text, use the Zoom Control at the bottom of the window to increase the magnification, as shown here.

Start Word and Enter Some Text

(continued)

③ If you are already working in Word, start a new document by clicking the File tab and clicking New. Click Blank Document and click Create.

④ In the blank document, click the Show/Hide tool in the Paragraph group of the Home tab. This shows paragraph marks, spaces, and tabs in your text as you type.

⑤ Type your text. When you reach the end of a line, keep typing. Word automatically moves, or *wraps*, the text to the next line.

⑥ Press Enter to begin a new paragraph.

See Also

"Correcting Your Spelling and Grammar" on pages 50–51 for information about working with the spelling and grammar checkers.

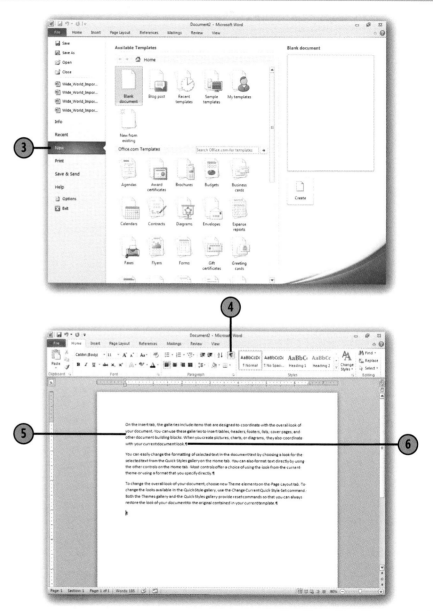

Save the Document

① Click the Save button on the Quick Access Toolbar.

② Choose a folder where you want to store the file, or if you want to save the file to your default location, click Hide Folders.

③ Type a name for the document in the File Name box. File names can be as long as 250 characters and can include spaces, but you can't use the \ / * ? <>or | characters.

④ Click Save.

⑤ Continue working on the document, saving your work frequently by clicking the Save button or pressing the keyboard shortcut Ctrl+S.

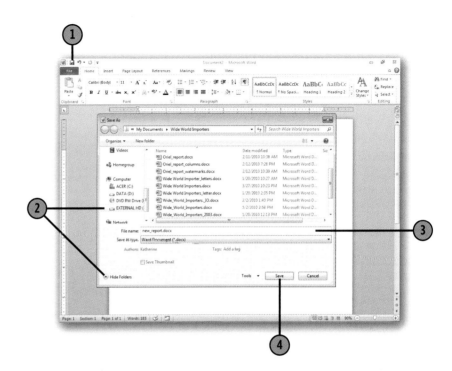

Tip

After you've saved your document for the first time, the Save As dialog box won't appear for subsequent saves. To save the document using a different location, name, or file format, click the File tab and click the Save As button.

See Also

"Word's File Formats" on pages 158–159 for information about using a different file format to save your document.

Starting with a Template

But there's no reason that you have to begin every new document as a blank page. Word 2010 comes with literally dozens of templates you can use to create brochures, letters, newsletters, postcards, flyers, and more. And because the templates that appear in Word come from Office.com, you've got an almost inexhaustible supply of new looks and styles always available for exploring.

Choose Your Template

1 Click File to display Backstage view and choose New.

2 Click the category of the templates you want to view by performing one of the following actions:

- Click Recent Templates to see the templates that you've used recently and double-click the one you want to use.

- Click Sample Templates to view templates Word 2010 offers as samples, showing examples of letters, reports, resumes, and more. Double-click one to open a new file based on the template.

- Click My Templates to display the New dialog box and your custom templates. Double-click a template to create a document.

- In the Office.com area, click an icon to display the templates in that category that are available for download and double-click the one you want to use.

- Click New From Existing to display the Open dialog box so that you can open an existing document as a template.

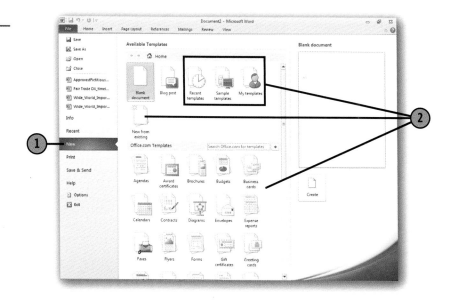

(continued on next page)

3 In the template category, click the template you want to view.

4 Click the Create button or the Download button to open the new document.

Tip

The new document you create is based on the template you selected; it is not actually the template file itself. In the new document, replace any placeholder text with your own text, and add any other elements you want your document to include.

Working with an Existing Document

Of course, not every document you work on will be a document you create from scratch. A friend asks you to proofread her newsletter. The president of the garden club asks you to add some text to the brochure. You decide to update your resume. Working with an existing document is as easy as opening the file, making your changes and additions, saving the document, and closing it until the next time you need it.

Open a Document

1. Click the File tab and click Open.
2. Click the folder in which the file is stored.
3. Click the file you want to open.
4. Click Open.

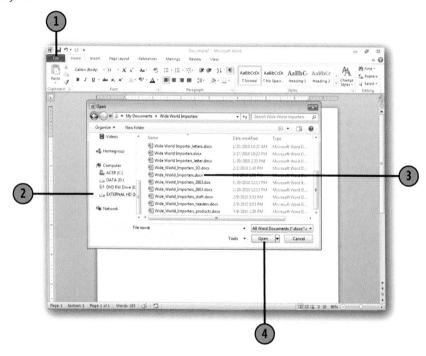

Tip

To open a document as a copy or as a read-only file, click the File tab and click Open; then choose the folder you need and click the file you want to open. Click the down arrow at the right of the Open button, and choose the option you want from the menu. Read-only lets you open the document but doesn't allow you to save it to the same folder using the same file name.

See Also

"Editing Your Content" on page 29 for information about selecting, deleting, replacing, and moving text.

Introducing Backstage View

Word 2010 offers all the tools you need to create, save, share, and choose options for your Word operations in Backstage view, which appears when you click the File tab. This convenient view gives you an easy way to create, open, and save files; get information about your document; find files you've used recently; and save and send the files you create.

When you click the File tab, Backstage view opens, and the Info tab is displayed. This tab displays the file's properties and authors, and gives you access to the commands you need to set permissions, prepare to save the file, and work with file versions. Other tabs in Backstage view—such as Recent, New, Print, and Save & Send—give you access to existing and new files and help you print and share the files you create. Additionally, you set program options and get Help in Backstage view.

Open Recently Used Files

① Click File to display Backstage view.

② Click Recent.

③ Click the file you want to open.

④ You can also click a folder to display the Open dialog box and navigate to the file you want to open.

Tip

To "pin" a specific file or folder to the displayed list in the Recent tab, click the small push pin icon to the right of the file name. This saves the item with the list so that each time you want to locate that file or folder you can see it in the Recent tab list. To "unpin" the item, simply click the icon a second time.

Find File and Program Information

1 Click File to display Backstage view.

2 In the Info tab, review file properties.

3 Choose the tools you want to work with in the center of the Backstage view window.

Click to display the properties dialog.

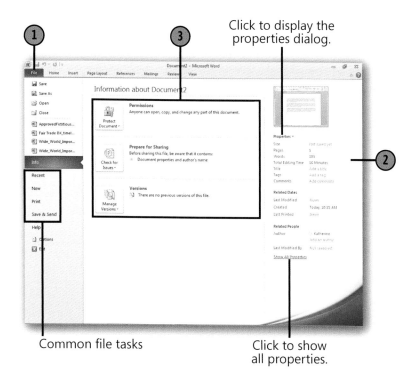

Common file tasks

Click to show all properties.

Click Manage Versions in the Info tab of Backstage view and choose Recover Draft Versions. A dialog box opens, showing unsaved versions of your file so that you can open and save the content. In this way you can recover information that you may have accidentally forgotten to save.

Tip

To close Backstage view and return to your file, click the File tab a second time.

Adding Content

One of the great things about Word 2010 is its flexibility. You can add content by typing your text, copying and pasting, inserting existing text files, or even dragging and dropping information to your open document page. What's more, you can use Word 2010's improved inking tools to write or sketch on your Word page.

Drag and Drop Text

① With both files open on your screen, select the information you want to add to your Word document.

② Drag the selected information to Word.

③ When the insertion point is positioned where you want to add the text, release the mouse button, and the text is added.

Tip ✓

If you're dragging and dropping content from Excel 2010 to Word 2010, press and hold Ctrl while you drag if you want to leave a copy of the information in the Excel workbook. Otherwise, the information will be moved from Excel into your Word document.

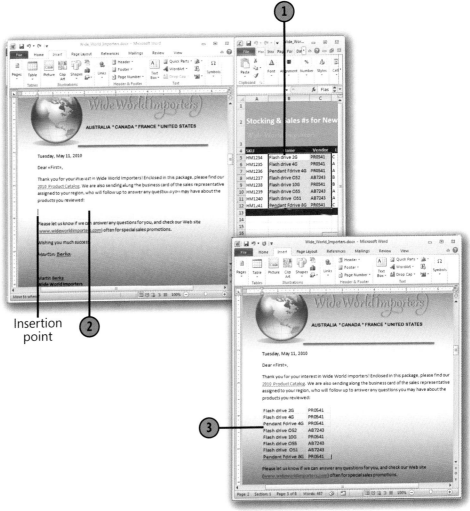

Insertion point ②

Insert a Text File

① Click to position the cursor in your document at the point you want to add the text file.

② Click the Insert tab, and in the Text group, click Object in the bottom-right corner of the Text group.

③ Click Text From File.

④ In the Insert File dialog box, find the file you want to insert.

⑤ Click Insert.

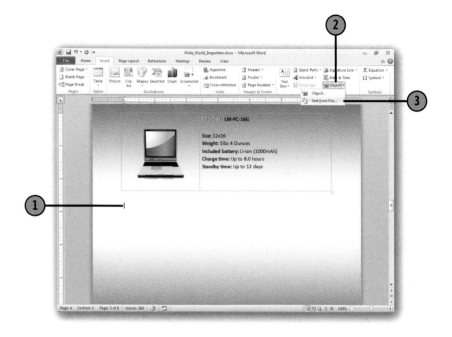

Use Ink to Add Content

① Display the page on which you want to add ink notes.

② Click the Review tab.

③ Click Start Inking.

④ Choose the pen style, ink, and thickness you want to use.

⑤ Write on your Tablet PC or drawing tablet as needed.

Tip

In addition to these methods of adding text to your blossoming document, you can also create and insert building blocks of text you use often in the documents you prepare. For more about working with building blocks, see page 48.

See Also

For the specifics on copying and pasting or moving text in a document, see page 44.

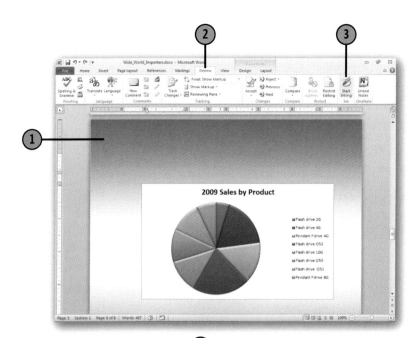

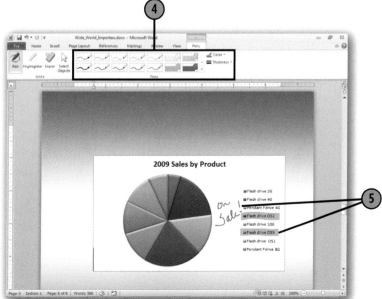

Adding Hyperlinks

You can add links in your document to make it easy for your readers to move from one document, file, or Web page to the next. You can create links, also called *hyperlinks*, to different parts of your document, to other Word documents, or to other types of files in an online document.

Link to an Item in Your Document

1 Select the text you want to use as a hyperlink.

2 On the Insert tab, click the Hyperlink tool in the Links group to display the Insert Hyperlink dialog box.

3 Click Place In This Document to see the headings and bookmarks that are contained in the document.

4 Click the heading or bookmark you want to link to.

5 Click the ScreenTip button, type a short description of the link that will appear when someone points to the hyperlink, and then click OK.

6 Click OK.

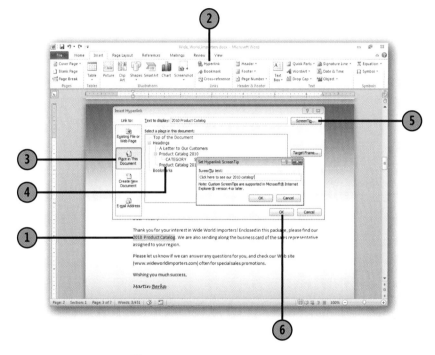

Tip

In many instances, Word can automatically insert hyperlinks—for example, when you create a table of contents, a table of figures, a table of equations, or a table of tables; or when you create cross-references, footnotes, and a master document. Take a look through this book to find examples of these automatically inserted hyperlinks.

Link to a Different Document

1. Type and select the text you want to use as a hyperlink.

2. On the Insert tab, click the Hyperlink tool in the Links group.

3. In the Insert Hyperlink dialog box, click Existing File Or Web Page.

4. Click a category to locate the file you want to link to:

   • Current Folder for a file in your default document folder or to locate a file in another folder on your computer or network

   • Browsed Pages for Web pages you've visited or files you've opened

   • Recent Files for files you've used recently

5. Use the Browse tools to locate a Web page or to move to the correct folder if the file is in a different folder.

6. Enter the Web address or click the file or the Web page you're linking to.

7. Click ScreenTip, type a short description of the link, and click OK.

8. Click OK.

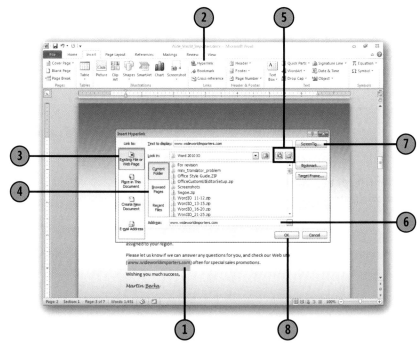

Tip ✓

Unless you enter some descriptive text in the ScreenTip dialog box, the ScreenTip will display the entire path and file name of the document, which usually isn't useful and doesn't describe the content.

Tip ✓

Want a quick way to display the Insert Hyperlink dialog box? Pressing Ctrl+K does the trick.

Tip ✓

By default, you must hold down the Ctrl key and click a hyperlink to use the link. Requiring the use of the Ctrl key to follow a hyperlink prevents unintended jumps and simplifies selecting a hyperlink for editing. If you prefer to follow a hyperlink without using the Ctrl key, click the Office button; click the Word Options button; and in the Advanced category of the Word Options dialog box, clear the Use CTRL+Click To Follow Hyperlink check box.

Printing a Document

The print process in Word 2010 is much easier, thanks to Back-stage view. Now you can preview your document as it will look when printed, set your print options, and print the file, all in a single view. You can also print your file directly to a OneNote notebook, if you use one to gather notes.

Preview Your Document

1. Click the File tab to display Backstage view and click Print.

2. Scroll through the document, using the page controls or the vertical scroll bar.

3. Use the Zoom slider to change your view of the document. Choose a specific zoom setting by clicking the Zoom tool and choosing the zoom percentage you want in the Zoom dialog box. Click OK.

4. If you're not happy with the way the document looks, click the Page Setup link to display the Page Setup dialog box and make the changes you want in the layout. Click OK.

Tip

If you're using a mouse with a scroll wheel, turn the wheel to move through the pages of Print Preview.

Print the Document

1 Click the File tab and choose Print.

2 Choose the printer you want to use.

3 Specify whether you want to print the entire document, a single page, some selected text, or a range of pages.

4 Specify the number of copies you want.

5 If you're printing multiple copies, specify whether the pages are to be printed in order (collated) or whether all copies of the same page are to be printed at one time.

6 Specify a scaling size if you want to print on paper that's a different size from the paper the document was originally set up for.

7 Choose the number of pages you want to print on a single page.

8 Click Print to print the document.

Tip ✓

To print special material—for example, a list of markups in the document, document properties, styles, or shortcut-key assignments—choose the item you want to print by clicking the arrow of the first item in the Settings area. Scroll down the list and click the item you want to print.

Tip ✓

You can print a document directly to a OneNote notebook by clicking the Printer setting arrow and choosing Send To One-Note 2010. When the Selection Location in OneNote dialog box appears, choose the notebook and section where you want to insert the document and click OK.

Getting Help

All the Word help you need is also within clicking distance in Backstage view. The Help tab provides you with information about your version of Word (which you'll need if you contact tech support at any point), as well as a link to get program updates and tools to display searchable help.

Browse for Help

1. Click the File tab to display Backstage view and click Help.

2. Click Check For Updates to make sure you have the most recent program updates.

3. Click Microsoft Office Help to display the Word Help dialog box.

4. Type a word or phrase and click Search to find help on a selected topic.

5. Click a link to display an article with help information.

6. If the font size is too small or too large, click the Change Font Size button, and choose a font size from the menu.

7. To print the topic, click the Print button.

8. To return to either the list or the articles, click the Back button. To return to the list of categories, click the Back button again.

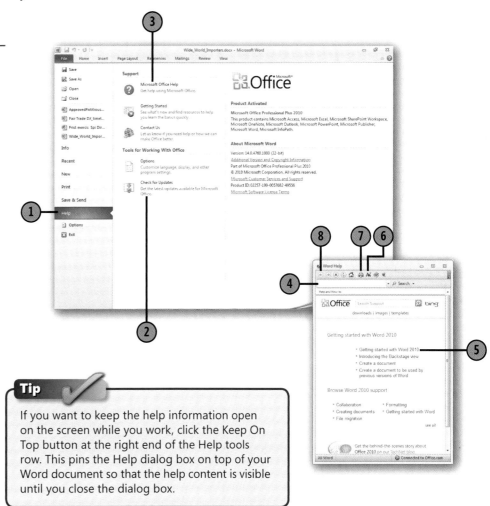

Tip

If you want to keep the help information open on the screen while you work, click the Keep On Top button at the right end of the Help tools row. This pins the Help dialog box on top of your Word document so that the help content is visible until you close the dialog box.

3

Editing Your Content

Once you've added content to your Word document, you need to know how to correct and fine-tune what you've created, whether your document is a letter, a report, a book chapter, a postcard, or something else entirely. Microsoft Word 2010 makes it easy for you to edit in the way that suits you best by enabling you to be flexible in the way you select and work with the text in your document. You can use the mouse or the keyboard to select text, make corrections, and navigate through your document.

Some of the most common editing practices include correcting words and phrases, checking spelling, reviewing your grammar, and updating or revising text. You may also need to translate words, phrases, or entire documents (something Word 2010 is particularly good at); insert special characters; or add, edit, and arrange the page numbers on the page.

Editing Basics

Some of the editing you do will be very simple; you'll simply need to click and press the Delete key or retype information you've already added. In other situations, you may need to replace whole paragraphs, sections, or pages of content. You can use both the mouse and the keyboard to select the text you want to edit.

Select and Modify Text

① Click at the beginning of the text that you want to select.

② Drag the mouse over the text to select it, and then release the mouse button.

③ Press the Delete key. The selected text is deleted.

④ Select some text that you want to replace with new typing.

⑤ Type the new text. The selected text is automatically deleted and replaced by the new typing.

⑥ Click Save.

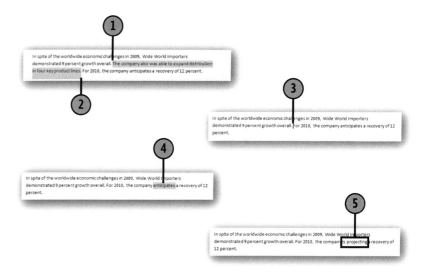

See Also

"Editing Your Way" on page 34 for more information about different ways to select text.

Tip

If you prefer to type over text without selecting it, you can use Overtype mode to replace text as you type. To turn Overtype mode on, click the File tab and click Options. Click Advanced and select the Use The Insert Key To Control Overtype Mode check box. Click OK, and then press the Insert key to turn on Overtype mode; press Insert again to turn off overtyping.

Tip

If you accidentally delete some text, immediately click the Undo button on the Quick Access Toolbar to restore the deleted text. You can also press Ctrl+Z to undo the action.

Use Keyboard Shortcuts

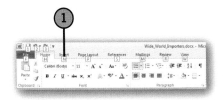

① Press Alt to display KeyTips for each tab and tool on the ribbon. After you press the key, additional KeyTips appear for the tools on the tab you selected.

② Press F6 to select an item on the status bar, and use the arrow keys to move from item to item.

③ Use the shortcut keys in the following table to complete various editing tasks.

If you decide you don't want to execute an action after you've pressed the Alt key, press the Esc key to return to your work.

"Getting Help" on page 27 for information about using Word Help.

Common Keyboard Shortcuts

Action	Keyboard Shortcut
Copy and delete (cut) selected content	Ctrl+X
Copy selected content	Ctrl+C
Paste content	Ctrl+V
Hide or minimize ribbon	Ctrl+F1
Apply/remove bold formatting	Ctrl+B
Apply/remove italic formatting	Ctrl+I
Apply/remove underline formatting	Ctrl+U
Align paragraph left	Ctrl+L
Align paragraph center	Ctrl+E
Align paragraph right	Ctrl+R
Add/remove space before paragraph	Ctrl+0 (zero)
Apply double-line spacing	Ctrl+2
Apply single-line spacing	Ctrl+1

Action	Keyboard Shortcut
Apply Normal style	Ctrl+Shift+N
Apply Heading 1 style	Alt+Shift+1
Apply Heading 2 style	Alt+Shift+2
Apply Heading 3 style	Alt+Shift+3
Change case	Shift+F3
Undo last action	Ctrl+Z
Redo last action	Ctrl+Y
Open shortcut menu	Shift+F10
Check spelling	F7
Save document	Ctrl+S
Save As	F12
Print (show Print dialog box)	Ctrl+P
Open Help	F1

Changing Your View

As you learned in the last chapter, Word 2010 offers a number of different views that enable you to get a fresh perspective on the document you're creating. Depending on what you want to do—produce a print document, create a Web page, design the outline of a long report—the different views help you get your work done efficiently and effectively. The view controls are located in the bottom-right corner of the Word window, and you can switch from view to view easily by simply clicking the icon of the view you want to use. You can also use the tools in the View tab to set and fine-tune the display in the various Word views.

Set the View

(1) In any view other than Full Screen Reading view, click the View tab.

(2) Choose the view you want to use.

(3) Click to display the Ruler, Gridlines, and the Navigation Pane.

(4) Click to set the display size of the page.

(5) Click to arrange the way open windows are displayed.

(6) Click to minimize the ribbon to get the maximum amount of room on the screen. Click a second time to return the ribbon to full display, or double-click a tab.

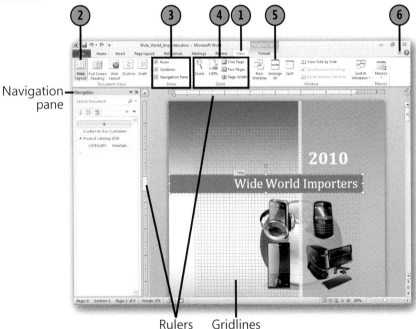

Navigation pane

Rulers   Gridlines

Tip ✓

You can also change the magnification by dragging the Zoom Control slider at the bottom-right of the window or by clicking the plus or minus signs next to the Zoom Control slider. You can also change the magnification by holding down the Ctrl key and turning the wheel on your mouse.

Tip ✓

Print Layout, Web Layout, and Draft views all offer similar tools in the ribbon, enabling you to control whether rulers and gridlines are displayed, how much you want the page to be magnified in the view, and how the windows are arranged. Full Screen Reading view and Outline view offer different tools that enable you to customize those particular views.

Editing Your Way

Word 2010 offers you a variety of ways to do most things. You might, for example, click a button, choose a list item, press a keyboard shortcut, select an item in a gallery, or click the mouse to accomplish the same result. Why are there so many choices? Well, one reason is that we all work differently. Given several choices, we usually do some experimenting, find the way that works best for us, and then use that method. Another reason is that different techniques work best in different situations.

Selecting text and then moving or copying it are a few of those procedures that offer different routes to the same end, and because choosing the best method can make a difference in how well your document goes together, this section offers a few tips about what to use when.

Try these common methods of selecting text to see which work best for you. Of course, there are other ways to select text, and, depending on whether and how you've customized Word, some selection methods might work a bit differently from those described here.

The process of moving or copying contents uses different tools, depending on what you want to do. When you use the F2 key or the Shift+F2 shortcut key, the selected material is stored in Word's short-term memory, where it's remembered only until you paste it into another location or do something else in Word.

The Cut and Copy tools in the Clipboard group of the Home tab enable you to store the selected material on the Office Clipboard, from where you can retrieve the information once or numerous times. The Office Clipboard stores up to 24 items, which you can retrieve one at a time or all at once.

Overwhelmed yet? There are still more ways to accomplish these same tasks! If you want to explore the full range of different ways to do these tasks, take a stroll through Word's Help and try out some of the other methods. The following table gives you an overview of the various ways you can perform simple text selection and editing tasks in Word 2010.

Cut

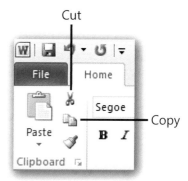

Copy

Tip

If you don't want to click the Copy tool in the Clipboard group of the Home tab, right-click the selected text and choose Copy, or press Ctrl+C.

See Also

For information about customizing Word, see the section "Customizing and Securing Word," starting on page 215.

See Also

For more information about using the Office Clipboard, see "Moving and Copying Text" on page 44.

Text-Selection Methods

To Select	Use this Method
Characters in a word	Drag the mouse over the characters.
A word	Double-click the word.
Several words	Drag the mouse over the words.
A sentence	Hold down the Ctrl key and click anywhere in the sentence.
A line of text	Move the pointer to the far left of the window and click when you see a right-pointing arrow.
A paragraph	Move the pointer to the far left of the window and double-click when you see a right-pointing arrow.
A long passage	Click at the beginning of the passage, and then hold down the Shift key and click at the end of the passage.
Noncontiguous blocks of text	Drag the mouse to select the first block. Hold down the Ctrl key and drag the mouse to select the second block.
A vertical block of text	Click at the top-left corner of the text block. Hold down the Alt key and drag the mouse over the text block.
The entire document	Press Ctrl+A.

Copying and Moving Methods

To Do This	Use this Method After You've Selected the Text
Move a short distance	Drag the selection to the new location.
Copy a short distance	Hold down the Ctrl key, drag the selection to the new location and release the Ctrl key.
Move a long distance or to a different document or program	Click the Cut button, click at the new location, and click the Paste button. OR press Ctrl+X, click at the new location, and press Ctrl+V.
Copy a long distance or to a different document or program	Click the Copy button, click at the new location, and click the Paste button. OR press Ctrl+C, click at the new location, and press Ctrl+V.
Copy several items and insert all at one place	Click the Copy button, select the next item, click the Copy button again, and repeat to copy up to 24 items. OR hold down the Ctrl key, select multiple items, and then click the Copy button. Click at the new location, and then click the Paste All button on the Clipboard.
Move a long or short distance	Press the F2 key, click at the new location, and press Enter.
Copy a long or short distance	Press Shift+F2, click at the new location, and press Enter.

Navigating Through the Document

The new Navigation Pane in Word 2010 replaces the Document Map feature in previous versions, enabling you to easily search for specific text items, move through your document by clicking headings, or even see thumbnail images of the pages you're creating. This makes it easy to find what you need quickly as you review and edit the content in your document.

Navigate by Heading

① Click the View tab and click Navigation Pane in the Show group.

② Click the heading of the section you want to view.

③ Click to expand the section to display subheads.

④ Click to collapse a section and hide subheads.

⑤ Move among sections in your document by clicking Preview Heading or Next Heading.

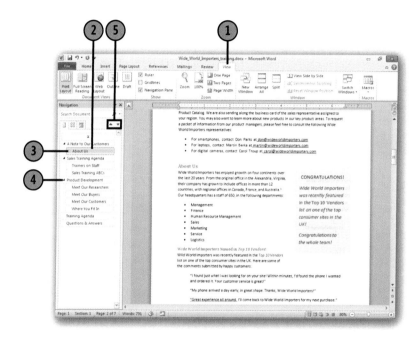

View Thumbnails

① Click the Browse The Pages In Your Document tab in the Navigation Pane.

② Scroll through the displayed thumbnails.

③ Click the page you want to display.

Tip

Reviewing thumbnails is a great way to get a last-minute look at the overall layout of your document. If you want to see whether you've used enough photos, for example, or you like the way the tables look, consider using the Navigation Pane to quickly skim all your pages at one time.

Search and Find Text

① Click the Browse The Results From Your Current Search tab in the Navigation Pane.

② Click in the Search box, type the word or phrase you're looking for, and press Enter.

③ Click the result you'd like to view.

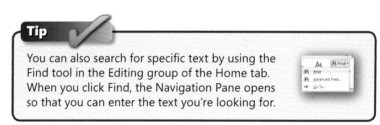

Tip

You can also search for specific text by using the Find tool in the Editing group of the Home tab. When you click Find, the Navigation Pane opens so that you can enter the text you're looking for.

Miss the Find And Replace Dialog Box?

If you want to work with the Find And Replace dialog box, simply press Ctrl+H to display it. Then you can click the tab you want (Find, Replace, or Go To) in order to carry out the particular editing operation you need to complete.

If you want to add special features to the text you're searching for—perhaps you want to ignore punctuation or find words that sound like the ones you're searching for—you can click the More button in the Find And Replace dialog box to set additional options.

Wildcards

"Wildcard" characters are used to represent other characters. The most commonly used wildcards are ? and *. The ? wildcard represents any single character, and the * wildcard represents any number of characters. For a complete list of wildcards, select the Use Wildcards check box, and click the Special button.

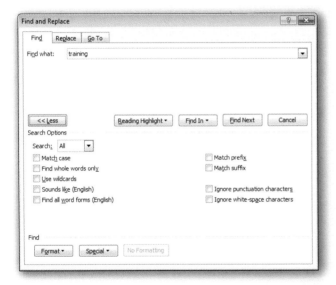

Converting Old Documents

Not every document you create will be a new document, of course. You might begin with last year's draft of the home show tour map and then modify it to fit this year's tour. When you open a document that was created in a version of Word prior to 2007, Word 2010 displays the document in Compatibility Mode. The upside is that your document will be compatible with files created in a pre-2007 version of Word. The downside is that many of the great new features—such as text effects and artistic elements—won't be available while you're working in that older format. You can convert the older document to take advantage of the new features and also point your older-model Word friends to a compatibility tool available online that will enable them to seamlessly read the documents you send—until they decide to upgrade for themselves.

Work in Compatibility Mode

1. Click the File tab and click Open to display the Open dialog box, and double-click the file to open it.

2. Work on the document as you normally would.

3. If you encounter a grayed (unavailable) feature such as Themes, simply ignore that feature because you can't use it.

4. Click the Save button to save the file in its original format.

The title bar indicates that you're working in Compatibility Mode.

Try This!

If you are working in a Word 2010 document and wonder which of the features you've used won't be available to friends and family working with an earlier version of Word, run the Compatibility Checker to find out. Click the File tab and in the Info tab, click Check For Issues. Click Check Compatibility, and the Microsoft Word Compatibility Checker displays all the features that will be impacted and enables you to choose the version of Word you want to use to compare.

Convert the Document

① With your Word 97–2003 format document open, click the File tab.

② In the Info tab, click Convert.

③ If you see a dialog box asking you whether you want to convert, click OK. The original file won't be overwritten because its file extension is different from that of the updated file.

④ Work on your document using all the features in Word.

Caution

If you upgrade the file format of the document, the file won't be usable by people who have earlier versions of Word unless they've installed the Office Compatibility pack, which enables them to read and save this type of file.

Tip

If you need to send an upgraded file to someone who has an earlier version of Word but doesn't have the Office Compatibility pack, point to the arrow at the right of the Save As command on the Office menu, and choose Word 97–2003 Document from the gallery that appears. You might lose some advanced features in that version of the document, but at least other people will be able to read it.

Tip

Some features work differently in Compatibility Mode than they do in Word 2010 format. For example, equations are inserted as pictures, and SmartArt graphics are limited to the diagrams used in earlier versions of Word. These modifications are necessary so that you can open the file in your earlier version of Word.

Reading a Document

In some cases, you just need to read through a document so that you can prepare for an upcoming meeting, learn about a new topic, or provide feedback to someone who has requested it. You can use Word's Full Screen Reading View to read the document in a view that is optimized to help you navigate easily while you read. You can also add comments, highlight words and phrases, and change the view to suit your style.

Read Through a Document

① Click the View tab and click Full Screen Reading.

② Click the arrow at the bottom-left corner of the page to move to the previous page or pair of pages, or click the right arrow to move to the next page or pair of pages.

③ Open the View Options menu, and choose

- Increase Text Size or Decrease Text Size to change the size of the screen text.

- Show One Page or Show Two Pages to view a single page or a pair of pages.

- Show Printed Page to view the page as it will look when printed, and Margin Settings to specify whether the margins should be shown correctly or shrunk so that the text can be shown in a larger size.

- Allow Typing to edit the text as you read it, and Track Changes to mark all changes.

- Show Comments And Changes to display all comments and marked changes, and to indicate which types of changes came from which reviewers.

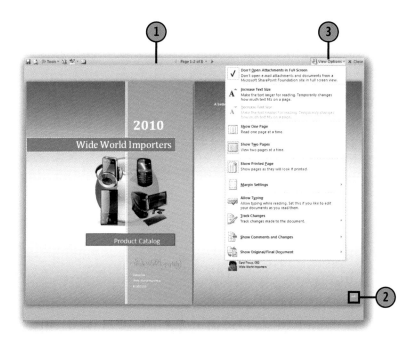

Tip

Word is set to display any Word attachments in your e-mail in Full Screen Reading view. If you prefer not to use this view, you can turn it off on the View Options menu.

Navigate the Document

(1) Click the Page button at the top of the document.

(2) Click your choice to move to a specific page, location, or heading, or to display the Navigation Pane.

(3) Click Find to display the Search tab of the Navigation Pane so that you can search for specific words or phrases.

(4) When you've finished, press the Esc key or click the Close button to exit Full Screen Reading view.

Tip

You can also use the choices in the Tools menu to highlight text, translate words and phrases, and look up more information about the topic.

See Also

"Working with Revision Marks" on page 206 for information about adding comments or tracking changes.

Moving and Copying Text

Word uses the *Clipboard* to temporarily store text and other content that you want to move or copy to another part of your document, to another document in the same program, or to a document in another program. You simply place your content on the Clipboard and then, when you're ready, you retrieve it by pasting it into its new location. Word uses two different Clipboards: the Windows Clipboard, which stores only the item most recently cut or copied; and the Office Clipboard, which can store as many as 24 different items, including the most recently cut or copied item, but which works only with Office programs. Word 2010 includes a dramatically improved feature called Paste with Live Preview that gives you choices about the way you paste information you've cut or copied.

Cut or Copy Text

(1) Select the text you want to cut or copy.

(2) Do either of the following:

- Click the Cut button in the Clipboard group of the Home tab (or press Ctrl+X) to delete the selected text and store it on the Clipboard.

- Click the Copy button (or press Ctrl+C) to leave the selected text in your document and place a copy on the Clipboard.

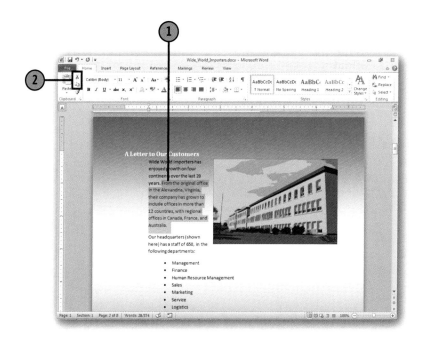

Paste the Cut or Copied Text

① Click in your document where you want to insert the text.

② Click the Paste button (or press Ctrl+V).

③ Point to the Paste option you want to use to preview it in your document. You may see the following choices:

- Keep Source Formatting preserves the format of the original copied text.

- Merge Formatting matches the format of the text surrounding the pasted text.

- Keep Text Only places only the text at the cursor position.

④ If you want to change the format of the pasted text, click the Paste Options button that appears and choose Match Destination Formatting from the menu.

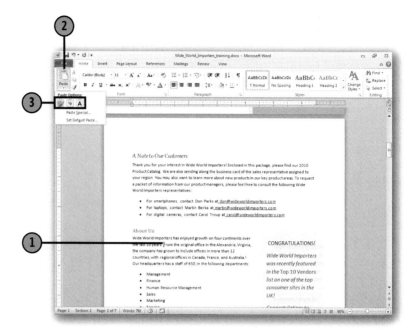

Copy and Paste Multiple Items

(1) Click the dialog launcher in the Clipboard group.

(2) Click each item you want to paste into the document and choose Paste.

(3) To paste all the items you copied into one location, click Paste All.

(4) Click Clear All when you no longer need any of the copied items and want to empty the Clipboard to collect and store new items.

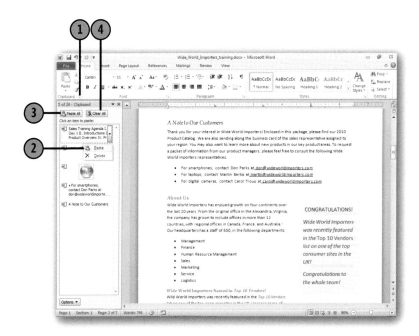

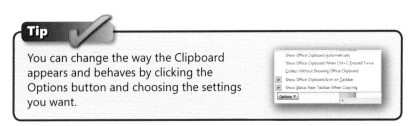

Replacing Text

Earlier in this section you saw the Find And Replace dialog box, an old standby for finding and changing words and phrases in your document. When you need to replace text in several places in your document, you can let Word do it for you to save time and trouble. It's a great way to use Word's speed and power to make quick work of those tedious document-wide changes.

Replace Text

(1) On the Home tab, click the Replace tool in the Editing group (or press Ctrl+H) to display the Find And Replace dialog box with the Replace tab selected. Click the More button to show the full dialog box.

(2) Type the text you want to find.

(3) Type the replacement text.

(4) To narrow the search, click Format and specify the formatting of the text you're searching for.

(5) To replace nontext items, click Special and specify any element that's associated with the text.

(6) Click one of the following:

- Replace to replace the found text and find the next instance of the search text.

- Replace All to replace all instances of the search text with the replacement text.

- Find Next to find the next instance of the search text without replacing it.

(7) Click Close when you've finished (the Cancel button changes to Close after you've conducted a search).

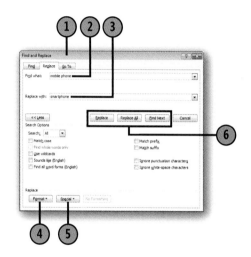

Tip

If you used the Replace All button and the results aren't what you expected, click the Undo button on the Quick Access Toolbar. You can then try the replacement again, this time with more specific search parameters.

Inserting Building Blocks

If you type the same word or phrase repeatedly, you can save yourself a lot of time (especially if you use long technical terms or difficult names) by saving that word or phrase as a building block that is available in your Quick Parts gallery. You assign the Quick Part a short name—a nickname of sorts, with at least four letters; then when you type the nickname, the Quick Part is inserted into your document. And the Quick Parts feature isn't limited to text; the information can be anything you can put into a document: pictures, tables, whole new pages, even fields. Word comes already equipped with numerous Quick Parts entries for some of the most common types of information you may want to add to your document.

Create a Building Block

1. In your document, select the content you want to use to create a building block. You might choose your mission statement, for example, or a quote you use on all your correspondence.

2. On the Insert tab, click the Quick Parts tool in the Text group, and choose Save Selection To Quick Part Gallery (or press Alt+F3) to display the Create New Building Block dialog box.

3. Accept the suggested name or type a new name for the entry.

4. Select Quick Parts if it isn't already displayed in the Gallery list.

5. Select a category for the entry, or choose Create New Category to create and select an additional category.

6. Specify where you want to save the entry: in the current template, the global Normal template, or the global Building Blocks collection.

7. Specify the way you want the material to be inserted.

8. Click OK.

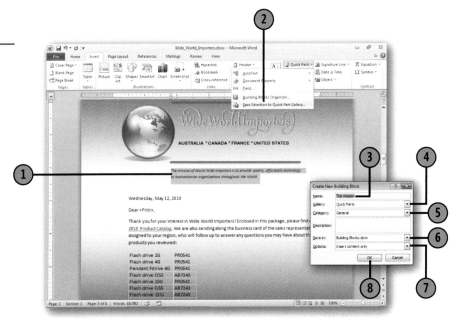

Tip

You can use Quick Parts to create, store, and retrieve many different types of content. In addition to text, you can store and retrieve cover pages, formatted pages, equations, and many other items.

Insert the Information

① Place the insertion point where you want the content to be inserted, type the name you assigned to the Quick Part you created, and press the F3 key to insert the content.

② Check your document to verify that Word inserted the correct information.

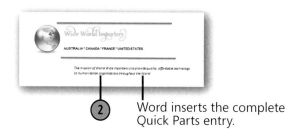

Word inserts the complete Quick Parts entry.

Tip

If you frequently use the Quick Parts gallery to insert content, open the gallery, right-click it, and choose to add the gallery to the Quick Access Toolbar. That way, you'll be able to access the gallery while you're working on any command tab in Word.

Try This!

Type **sund** and press Enter to insert the AutoText "Sunday." This is just one example from Word's long list of built-in Quick Parts entries that frequently show up as AutoComplete entries.

Tip

The building block you added will also be available in the Quick Parts gallery, so you can add it to your document by clicking in the document, choosing Quick Parts, and clicking the building block in the gallery. You can also right-click the item in the gallery to choose where you want the item to be placed.

Correcting Your Spelling and Grammar

Your document may look and read great, but if there are mis-spellings sprinkled here and there, your readers are going to miss how great your document really is. Clean up any stray mistakes by using Word's Spelling and Grammar checker. Word 2010 points out any misspelled or unrecognized words and can even help you check the spelling of translated words and phrases. The Grammar checker helps you make sure that your text is readable and clear.

Correct a Spelling Error

① Right-click a red squiggle to see one or more suggestions for correcting the error.

② Click the suggestion you want to use.

③ If you believe that what you have isn't an error but is something that isn't recognized by Word, click Ignore or Ignore All to tell Word to ignore the word throughout this document, or click Add To Dictionary to have Word ignore the word throughout all your documents.

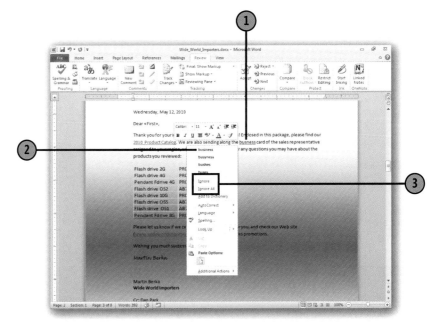

See Also

"Correcting Text Automatically" on page 52 for information about having Word automatically correct the spelling of words you frequently misspell and "Customizing Your Spelling Dictionaries" on page 225 for information about adding and modifying the dictionaries that are used in the spelling check.

Tip

If Word didn't offer any suggestions when you right-clicked a squiggle, return to your document and try to correct the error yourself. If the squiggle remains, right-click it and see whether there are any suggestions now.

Tip

To get correction suggestions and to correct errors using the keyboard, move the insertion point into the mis-spelled word, press the F7 key and use the Spelling And Grammar dialog box to make your changes.

Correct a Contextual Spelling Error

① Right-click a blue squiggle to see one or more suggestions for fixing improper word usage.

② Click the suggestion you want, or choose to ignore this error or this word throughout the document.

Tip

Word uses blue squiggles to mark formatting inconsistencies as well as contextual spelling errors.

Tip

If you chose to ignore misspelled words or improper grammar but you're now having second thoughts, click the File tab and click Options. Click Proofing and click the Recheck Document button to remove all your Ignore choices.

Correct the Grammar

① Right-click a green squiggle.

② If the shortcut menu suggests alternative phrasing, click to use the alternative. If only a description of the problem is shown, click in the document and edit the text as suggested.

③ If you're sure your grammar is correct, click Ignore Once.

④ If you want to know why the text was marked, click About This Sentence for an explanation of the grammar rules involved.

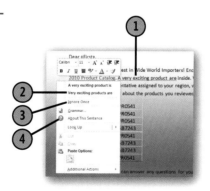

Try This!

In a document that has spelling and/or grammar errors, click the Proofing Errors icon on the status bar. Correct the error, and then click the icon again to find the next error. Continue finding and correcting your spelling and grammar errors until your document is error-free.

Correcting Text Automatically

So do you have a mental block when it comes to the spelling of certain words? Is it hard to remember "i before e except after c"? Word offers the AutoCorrect feature just for you. You can teach Word about your common misspellings and AutoCorrect will watch for the words and correct them for you.

Teach Word to Correct Your Misspellings

① Right-click one of your own common misspellings.

② Point to AutoCorrect on the shortcut menu and choose the correct spelling from the list of suggestions that appears.

③ Check your document and observe that the correct spelling has replaced your misspelling. Continue composing your document. Note that if the same misspelling occurs again, Word corrects it for you.

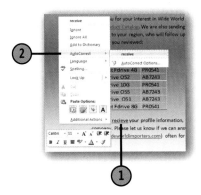

Add Other Entries

1. Click the File tab and click Options. In the Word Options dialog box, click Proofing.

2. Click the AutoCorrect Options button.

3. Make sure the Replace Text As You Type check box is checked in the AutoCorrect tab.

4. Enter the abbreviated or incorrect text that you'll type.

5. Type the text that you want to replace the text you typed.

6. Click Add.

7. Add other entries if desired. Click OK when you've finished.

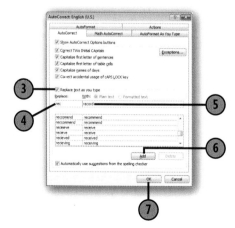

Control the Corrections

1. Click the File tab and click Options; click Proofing and click the AutoCorrect Options button.

2. On the AutoCorrect tab, select this check box to have AutoCorrect changes marked with the AutoCorrect Options button in your document so that you can reverse the changes if you want.

3. Select or clear check boxes to specify the items you want Word to correct.

4. Select this check box to have Word replace any item in the list with its correction.

5. Select this check box to have a misspelling automatically replaced with a correction from the spelling dictionary, if the correction is clear.

6. Click Exceptions to specify when a word that would normally start with a capital letter is *not* to be capitalized (for example, after the apparent end of a sentence or after a specified word or abbreviation), when two capitalized letters in a row are not to be corrected, and any other exceptions you want to add.

7. Click OK.

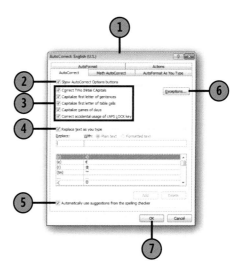

Tip

AutoCorrect remembers when you don't want it to change items such as the capitalization of the first letter in a sentence, or two initial capital letters. However, if you do want it to make these changes on a case-by-case basis, you have two choices. You can use the Backspace key to remove the correction and can then retype the text the way you want it (but for this to work, the Automatically Add Words To List check box must be selected in the AutoCorrect Exceptions dialog box), or you can click the AutoCorrect Options button for the correction and use the menu to prevent Word from making these corrections.

Researching a Subject

When you're working on your document and suddenly go blank, wouldn't it be great to be able to look up information that would help you get going again? Maybe a peek at a thesaurus will help. Or an interesting definition of a word will spark some new ideas. Word can help you expand your understanding when you use the built-in research features to find out more about the words you're using as you write about your chosen topic.

Do Some Research

① Click in a word (or select a group of words) that you want information about.

② On the Review tab, click the Research tool in the Proofing group.

③ Select the resource or the types of resources you want to use.

④ Review the results.

⑤ If you want to look up something more, type the word or words, and press Enter.

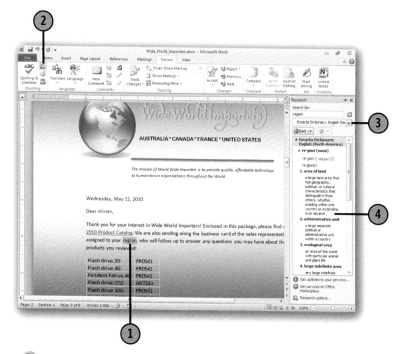

Tip

You can fine-tune the types of results Word displays in the Research task pane by clicking Research Options at the bottom of the pane. In the Research Options dialog box, click the services you want to include in your search; then click OK to save your changes.

Caution

Some research services charge to view the full content of their results. If there's a charge, you'll see an icon indicating the amount next to the search result.

Tip

To quickly open the Research task pane, hold down the Alt key and click the word to be looked up.

Translating Your Text

Today it's not unusual to be trading files with friends from other countries and including in your document phrases, places, and sayings that are common in other cultures. Word 2010 includes improved language tools that help you translate words or phrases as you go. The Mini Translator pops up over your document to provide quick translations within easy reach. And you can set your language preferences in proofing tools so that you can be sure you're using the phrases correctly no matter which language you're using.

Choose a Translation Language

① On the Review tab, click Translate in the Language group.

② Click Choose Translation Language.

③ In the Translation Language Options dialog box, click the Translate To arrow. This is the setting that controls what you see in the Mini Translator.

④ Select the language from which you want to translate.

⑤ Choose the language you want to translate to.

⑥ Click OK.

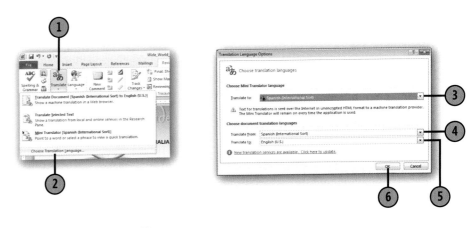

Tip

If you see a prompt at the bottom of the dialog box, click it to ensure that you have the most recent translation updates downloaded to your version of Word.

Use the Mini Translator

1. On the Review tab, click Translate in the Language group and click Mini Translator.

2. Select the text in your document you'd like to translate.

3. Hover the mouse pointer over the text, and the Mini Translator appears.

4. Click Expand to open the Translation page of the Research task pane so that you can find out more about the translation.

5. Click Copy to copy the translated text for pasting in another location.

6. Click Play to hear the translation pronounced.

7. Click Help to get more information about translation features.

8. Click Update Services to download translation updates to your version of Word.

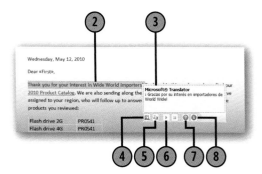

Tip

If you plan to use the Play feature so that you can hear the translation pronounced, be sure to have the volume on your computer turned on and set to an adequate level.

Formatting Documents

Your words may be engaging and brilliant, but if you cram a bunch of them on the page in no particular format, readers are going to look for something more inviting to read. The format of your documents goes a long way toward inviting the reader and holding his or her interest. Headlines let readers know what's most important on a page; readable body text is easy on the eye; bullet lists and numbered lists present information in bite-sized chunks. Pull quotes, captions, callouts, and more—as well as columns, borders, and spacing—all contribute to the reading experience your reader will have.

Microsoft Word 2010 includes a number of features that make formatting your documents a breeze. You can apply themes and styles to contr ol the overall font and color selections; adjust the spacing to give your text a little breathing room; and add borders, columns, and more to help lead the reader down the page. Whether you're creating letters, reports, memos, flyers, or a training manual, the formatting features in Word 2010 simplify the look of your document and help you make your point clearly and easily.

Formatting Documents with Themes, Styles, and Fonts

Most of us know what we like when we're looking at a document. We seem to instinctively know whether something will be easy (or worth it) to read. We like certain colors used together—we are drawn to some publications more than others. Designers seem to have a sixth sense about this kind of thing, understanding what fonts and colors promote the most pleasing reading experience for those of us reading their documents. Luckily, Word 2010 includes the wisdom and talent of designers in key formatting features that you can apply to your own documents. With Word 2010 formatting tools you can create consistent, easy-to-read pages that look professional and put-together for your readers. The following sections describe the various formatting features you're likely to use as you apply formats to your pages.

Themes

Themes are the controllers of your design. A theme coordinates the font, color scheme, and special effects for objects in your document, including the shading and shadow of shapes. When you change a theme, all the coordinated styles change, resulting in a whole new look for your document.

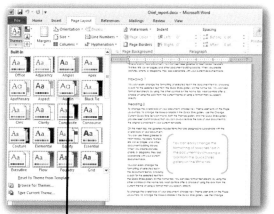

Point to a theme to see how it will look in your document.

Styles

Word 2010 offers a variety of styles that enable you to format different elements in your document:

- **Paragraph styles** define the layout of your paragraphs—line spacing, indents, tab spacing, borders, and so on.

- **Character styles** define the look of individual text characters—for example, boldfaced, italicized, or underlined emphasis; strikethrough, superscript, color, and shadow effects; and spacing between characters. If you specify the font as something other than the theme's default font, the character style can also define the font and font size. Otherwise, the font is determined by the chosen theme.

- **Linked styles** define both paragraph and character formatting. For example, in a single style you can define the paragraph layout, including the alignment and line spacing, as well as the appearance of the characters for the entire paragraph, including font, font size, emphasis, and effects.

- **Table styles** control the appearance of your tables—for example, the shading of rows or columns and the thickness of the gridlines.

- **List styles** determine the appearance of your bulleted and numbered lists—for example, the kind of bullet used and how far the paragraph is indented.

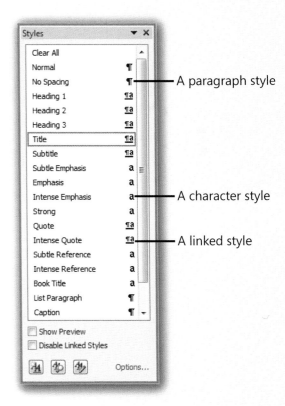

A paragraph style

A character style

A linked style

Direct Formatting

You can also use direct formatting to create customized words, paragraphs, or blocks of text. For example, you can apply bold formatting to a couple of words to make them stand out, or select a quotation and add italics to it. It's a good idea to use styles as much as possible so that you can maintain a consistent look, but you may want to directly format text in special instances. If you use direct formatting and later want to use the same formatting again, you can either use that formatting to create a new style or copy the formatting and apply it elsewhere with the Format Painter tool.

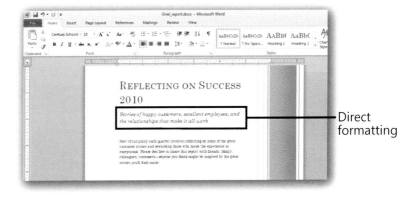

Direct formatting

Choosing and Changing Themes

Themes are the big formatting story in Word 2010. A theme is a coordinated set of fonts, colors, and special effects that are applied throughout your document automatically. When you choose a specific headline style, for example, the theme controls the font, size, color, and effect of the text. If you decide to choose a different theme later, the elements that are connected to that theme—headings, body text, object effects, and more—change to reflect the new theme automatically. In this way, Word 2010 makes creating and formatting documents more flexible and easier than ever.

Preview and Choose a Theme

① Open the document you want to use.

② Click the Page Layout tab.

③ Click the Themes arrow and choose any of the following:

- Point to a theme to see how your document will look if you use that theme.

- Click Reset To Theme From Template to revert to the original theme for the document.

- Click Browse For Themes to display the Choose Theme Or Themed Document dialog box. Select a theme or a document that contains the theme you want and click Open.

④ Click the theme you want to apply.

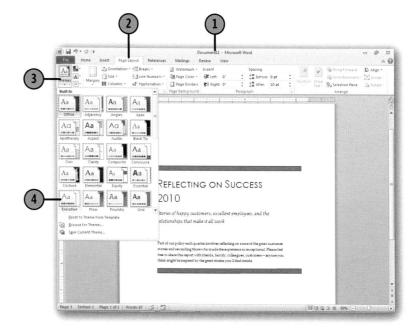

Tip

The Styles available in the Styles group of the Home tab reflect the theme you've chosen in the Themes group of the Page Layout tab. If you choose a different theme, the styles in the Styles gallery change.

Tip

After you apply and work with a theme in your document, another option becomes available on the Themes list. Save Current Theme enables you to save the theme to the Themes gallery so that you can use it for other documents you create.

Change the Theme

① Click the Page Layout tab.

② Click the Themes arrow.

③ Click the new theme. The color scheme, fonts, and shape effects change automatically to reflect your new choice.

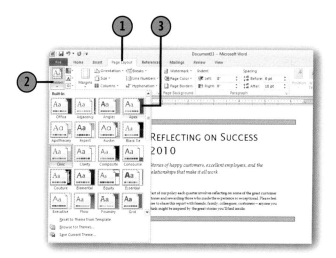

Caution

You can change the format—including the color and font—of items on your page, but be aware that doing so changes them from the default styles applied by the theme. This means that if you choose a new theme at a later time, the elements you formatted directly will not automatically change to reflect the new theme.

Modify a Theme

1. Click the Page Layout tab, click Theme Colors in the Themes group to display the gallery of color groupings, and click the color grouping you want.

2. Click Theme Fonts, and select the font pairing from the gallery that appears.

3. Click Theme Effects, and select the shadow and shading effects you want to use for shapes, SmartArt diagrams, and graphs.

4. Use the theme fonts, colors, and effects in your document.

5. If you like your customized theme, on the Page Layout tab, click the Themes tool and choose Save Current Theme. In the Save Current Theme dialog box, type a name for the theme, and click Save.

See Also

"Changing Style Sets" on page 68 for information about using different Quick Style sets for a theme.

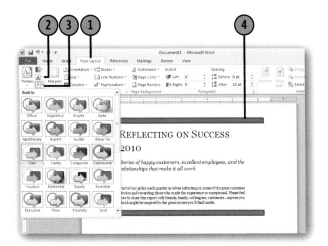

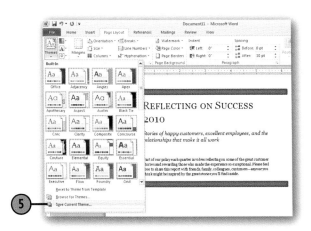

Applying and Saving Styles

Styles make it easy for you to coordinate the format of repeating elements in your document. This helps you keep things consistent by coordinating your text font, size, color, and so on. Word 2010 includes many predesigned styles as part of the program, and you can also create and modify styles to suit your own needs.

Choose a Style from the Gallery

1. Click in the text you want to format.
2. On the Home tab, click to display the Styles gallery.
3. Preview different styles and click the one you want to apply.

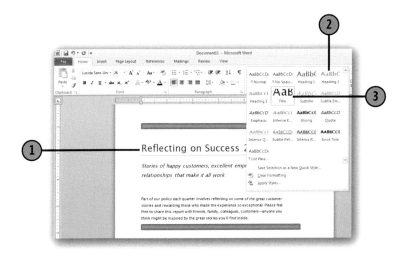

Try This!

Open the Quick Styles gallery and click Apply Styles to display the Apply Styles window. Click in a paragraph or select the text you want to format. Click the Apply Styles window and start typing the name of the style you want. Press Enter when the name of the style you want is displayed.

Apply a Style from the Styles Palette

① Click in the text you want to change.

② On the Home tab, click the dialog launcher in the Styles group.

③ Select the Show Preview check box if it isn't already selected.

④ Click the style you want to apply.

⑤ If the style you want isn't listed, click Options. In the Styles Pane Options dialog box, under Select Styles To Show, click All Styles, click OK, and then click the style you want.

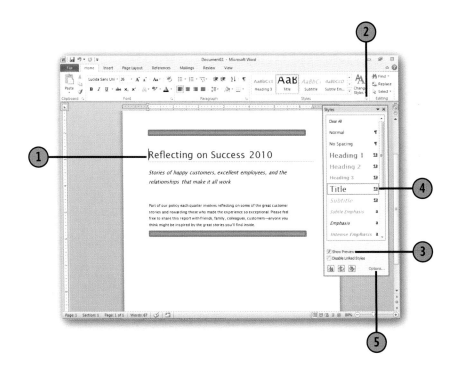

Tip

If you don't see any changes to the formatting of your paragraphs, you might not have the Live Preview feature enabled. To enable it, click the File tab and click Options. In the General category, click the Enable Live Preview check box, and click OK.

Tip

The symbol at the right of the style name indicates the style type: paragraph, character, or linked.

Changing Style Sets

A style set is a collection of style choices that reflect a particular mood or personality in your document. Is the tone of your document happy, somber, businesslike, or playful? You can choose a style set—or create one of your own—to give your text just the kind of look you're hoping for.

Select a Style Set

(1) On the Home tab, click the Change Styles tool in the Styles group.

(2) Point to Style Set and then point to the Quick Style set you want to see.

(3) Click a set to apply it or preview other styles until you find the one you want.

See Also

"Applying and Saving Styles" on page 66 for information on choosing a specific style you want to add to your text.

Tip

If you want this to be the style set you'll use in other documents based on this template, click Change Styles again and then choose Set As Default from the menu that appears.

Caution

If you are creating documents for business use, don't change the style set unless it's okay to change the font, style, and color scheme used for your business. Most businesses try to produce a coordinated look with their business communications, so make sure you have the necessary green light before you begin changing styles on the fly.

Formatting Text

In some cases you'll want simply to format a text phrase or selection that doesn't require choosing a theme or applying a style. This type of direct text formatting is simple in Word. You can quickly apply the format you want before you type the text, while you're typing, or after you've typed the words you want to format.

Apply Character Formatting

(1) Click the Home tab if it isn't already selected.

(2) Click in the text you want to format.

(3) Choose a formatting tool in the Font group to change the look of the selected text.

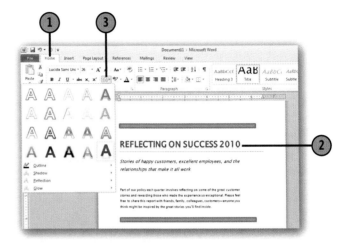

Text Formatting Tools

Tool	Name	Shortcut Key	Description
Calibri (Body) ▾	Font	Ctrl+Shift+F	Changes the font applied to the selected text
11 ▾	Font Size	Ctrl+Shift+P	Chooses a different font size for the text
$A^{\blacktriangle}$	Grow Font	Ctrl+>	Increases font size one point
$A^{\blacktriangledown}$	Shrink Font	Ctrl+<	Decreases font size one point
Aa ▾	Change Case		Changes lowercase to uppercase and vice versa
﹅	Clear Formatting		Removes all formatting of selected text
B	Bold	Ctrl+B	Applies a bold style to text
I	Italic	Ctrl+I	Italicizes selected text
U	Underline	Ctrl+U	Underlines selected text
a̶b̶c̶	Strikethrough		Adds the strikethrough style to text
x_2	Subscript	Ctrl+=	Formats the text as subscript
x^2	Superscript	Ctrl+Shift++	Formats the text as superscript
A ▾	Text Effects		Displays a gallery of text effects you can apply to your document
ab ▾	Text Highlight Color		Displays a palette from which you can choose a color to highlight text
A ▾	Font Color		Displays a palette from which you can choose a color for selected text

Creating a Bulleted or Numbered List

Although it is possible to go overboard with lists in a document, readers on the whole tend to appreciate them. Lists can provide small bits of information in an easy-to-understand format. Word 2010 makes formatting lists simple for you. Not only does Word add numbers or bullets to your list, with consistent spacing between the number or bullet and the text, it also keeps track of your list so that if you move an item within a numbered list, Word will renumber the list to keep the items in the correct order. You can also have the numbering skip paragraphs and can even split lists by restarting a series at 1.

Create a List

① Type the first line for your list. Make sure you're using the paragraph style you want for the list.

② On the Home tab, click the Numbering tool in the Paragraph group for a numbered list or the Bullets tool for a bulleted list.

③ After completing the first line, press Enter to start the second list item.

④ When you've completed the list, press Enter twice to create an empty paragraph and to turn off the list formatting.

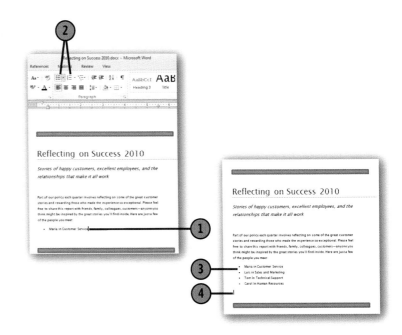

See Also

"Creating a Multilevel List" on page 75 for information about placing a list inside another list.

See Also

"Customizing a Bulleted or Numbered List" on page 73 for information about changing the look of a list.

Create a Discontinuous Numbered List

① Create the first part of the numbered list.

② Click the Numbering tool to turn off the numbers.

③ Type at least one non-list paragraph.

④ In a blank paragraph, click the Numbering tool to turn the numbers on again, click the AutoCorrect Options button that appears, and choose Continue Numbering from the drop-down menu.

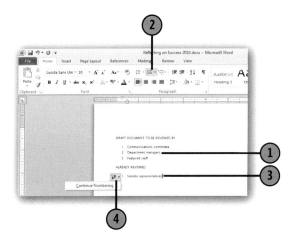

Modify the List

① Right-click in the list you want to change.

② From the shortcut menu, choose the action you want for that item in the list.

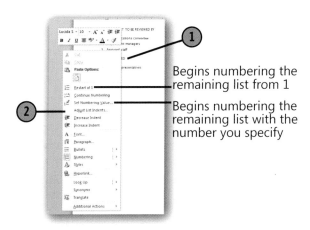

Begins numbering the remaining list from 1

Begins numbering the remaining list with the number you specify

Customizing a Bulleted or Numbered List

Although standard bullets or numbers may be fine for most lists, you might want to add some pizzazz to a special document with decorative bullets, or you might need to change your numbering format to conform to certain document specifications. Whatever the reason, you can customize the bullets and the numbering scheme for your lists.

Change the Bullets

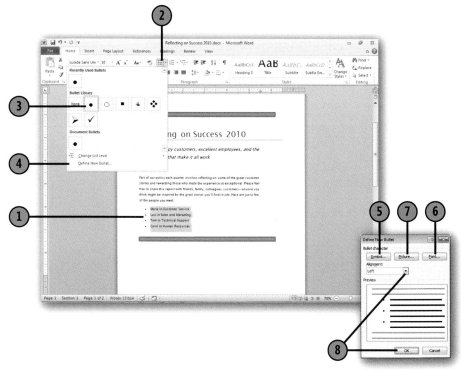

① Select the entire list if it's completed, or click in your document where you want to start a list.

② On the Home tab, click the Bullets arrow in the Paragraph group to display the Bullets gallery.

③ Click the bullet character you want to use.

④ If none of the displayed bullets is exactly what you want, click Define New Bullet at the bottom of the gallery to display the Define New Bullet dialog box.

⑤ To use a text symbol, or dingbat, as a bullet, click Symbol. In the Symbol dialog box, select the font and the symbol you want, and click OK.

⑥ To modify the size, color, or any other aspect of the symbol, click the Font tool, make your changes in the Font dialog box, and click OK.

⑦ To use a clip-art picture bullet, click Picture, choose the bullet you want in the Picture Bullet dialog box, and click OK.

⑧ Select the alignment of the bullet in relation to the table text, and click OK.

Tip

By default, the Include Content From Office Online check box is selected, which means that picture bullets from Office.com are included in the displayed gallery. If you don't see one to click, click in the Search box, type a word or phrase that describes what you're looking for, click Go, and then select the bullet you want from the displayed results.

Change the Numbering Scheme

(1) Select the list or click where you want to start a list.

(2) On the Home tab, click the Numbering arrow in the Paragraph group to display the Numbering gallery. If none of the available numbering formats is what you want, click Define New Number Format near the bottom of the gallery to display the Define New Number Format dialog box.

(3) Select the numbering style you want.

(4) Add any text that you want to be included in the numbering.

(5) Select the alignment of the numbering in relation to the table text.

(6) If you want to modify the font, size, color, or any other aspect of the numbering and any added text, click the Font tool, make your changes in the Font dialog box, and click OK.

(7) Use the preview to see the effect of the alignment and any changes you've made to the font settings.

(8) Click OK.

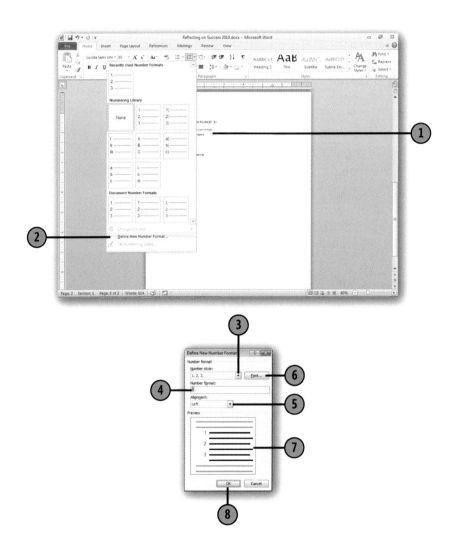

Creating a Multilevel List

Sometimes a regular list just won't do the job. If you need to create a list within a list (called a *nested* list), what you need is a way to create a multilevel list. Luckily, Word 2010 has just the tool to help you do that.

Create a Multilevel List

(1) Type the first line of your list.

(2) Click either the Numbering or the Bullets tool in the Paragraph group to choose the type of list you want.

(3) Continue creating the list of items that are all at the same level.

(4) At the beginning of the line where you want the second level to begin, press the Tab key. Type the item and press Enter. Continue entering the items that belong in this level of the list.

(5) At the beginning of the paragraph with which you want to start the third level of the list, press the Tab key again.

(6) To return to the second level of the list, press Shift+Tab. Press Shift+Tab a second time to move from the second level to the first level of the list.

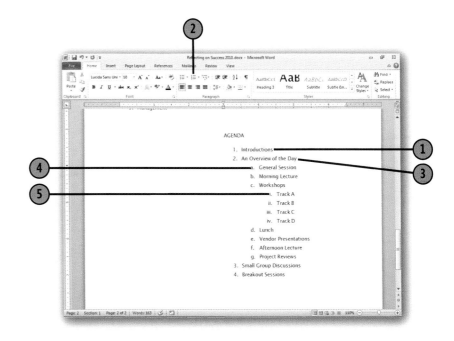

Tip

You can create a list with as many as nine levels. If you need more than nine levels, you might want to reconsider what you're trying to do in your list!

Choose a Multilevel List Style

① Type the first level of your list.

② Click the Multilevel List tool in the Paragraph group.

③ Choose the list style you want to apply to the multilevel list.

④ Type the additional items, pressing Tab before each item you want to format at a new level.

⑤ Press Shift+Tab to move the cursor one level toward the left margin.

If you don't like a sublevel's indent, point to the number or the bullet, and drag it to where you want the indent. All the items in the list at that level will move to the new indent.

Customizing a Multilevel List

A multilevel list is a powerful tool for presenting your information in an organized, hierarchical way. The multilevel lists that are available in the List Library provide some structure, but you might need to develop your own structure to present the information in exactly the way you want.

Create a List Structure

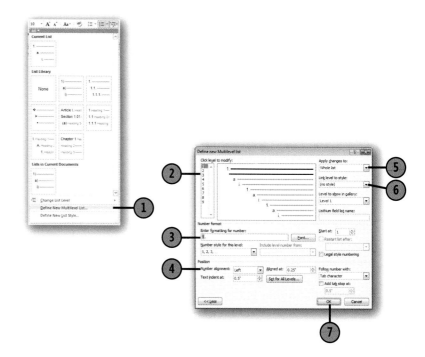

(1) Click the Multilevel List arrow, and click Define New Multilevel List near the bottom of the gallery to display the Define New Multilevel List dialog box. Click the More button, if it's displayed, to see all the settings. (The Less button is displayed when the More button has been clicked.)

(2) Click a list level that you want to modify.

(3) Define your numbering format. Add or edit any text that you want to use with the number; then specify the numbering style and the number with which that list level starts.

(4) Set the position of the numbering in relation to the text.

(5) Specify whether these changes apply to the entire list or only part of it.

(6) Specify which style you want to use with this level and what level you want assigned to this style when it's included in a list.

(7) Click OK.

Tip

In the gallery, click a multilevel list that's similar to the style you want before you start customizing the list. That way, you might not need to change every level of the list.

Changing Character Font and Size

The font and font size you choose for your document conveys a particular tone and feeling. Large elaborate fonts gush; small neat fonts speak more softly. The combinations you choose have a definite effect on how readers perceive your document. You can easily set both of these elements for all or part of your content with just a few clicks on the ribbon.

Change the Font

1 Select the text you want to change.

2 On the Home tab, click the Font arrow in the Font group.

3 Click the font from the displayed list.

Fonts recommended for the current theme

Fonts that you've used recently

List of all fonts

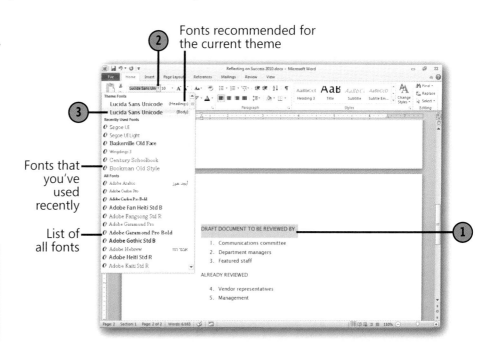

Tip

Use Quick Styles or custom styles to apply consistent font formatting for similar content throughout your document. Use direct formatting for special formatting or to design and create new styles.

Tip

You can also change the font and font size using the Mini toolbar that appears when you select some text and keep the mouse pointer pointing to the selected text.

Try This!

Create and select some text in your document. On the Home tab, click the Font list down arrow, point to a font, and drag your mouse slowly down the list. Note that the font of the selected text changes to the font you're pointing to. When you see the font you like, click it to use that font.

Change the Font Size

1. Select the text you want to change.
2. On the Home tab, do any of the following:
   - Click the Font Size arrow and click a size in the list.
   - Click the Font Size list, and type the font size you want.
   - Click the Grow Font tool or the Shrink Font tool to increase or decrease the font size.

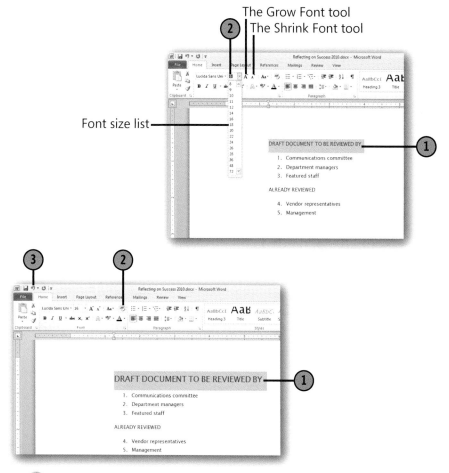

The Grow Font tool
The Shrink Font tool

Font size list

Restore the Default Font and Font Size

1. Select the text to which you want to restore the default settings for that style.
2. On the Home tab, click the Clear Formatting tool.
3. If you don't like the results, click the Undo tool on the Quick Access Toolbar and use the formatting tools to modify the formatting of the selected text.

See Also

"Modify a Theme" on page 65 for information about setting the default heading and body text fonts for your theme.

Caution

The Clear Formatting tool changes not only the font and font size but also any emphasis—bold, italic, or underline—that you have applied.

See Also

"Applying and Saving Styles" on page 66 for information about using existing formatting to create or modify a style.

Adjusting Paragraph Line Spacing

When you're so busy filling your page with text and formatting it, you may at first overlook the importance of the space in which the text sits. The amount of space surrounding your text is an important part of the overall design, and it has a lot to do with how readable your text is—or isn't. Too little space makes the lines of text looked squashed together and difficult to read; too much space also makes the text difficult to read because the reader's eye has to search for the beginning of the next line.

Set the Line Spacing Within a Paragraph

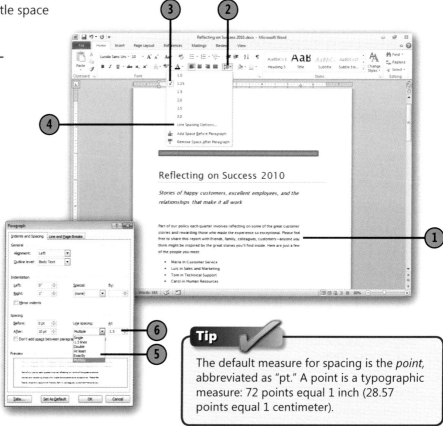

① Click in a paragraph or select the paragraphs with the line spacing you want to set.

② On the Home tab, click the Line Spacing tool in the Paragraph group.

③ Click the line spacing you want.

④ If you don't see the spacing you want, click Line Spacing Options.

⑤ In the Paragraph dialog box that appears, select the type of line spacing you want:

- Exactly to create a specific space between lines regardless of the font size used

- At Least to create a minimum space between lines, which can increase if large font sizes are used

- Multiple to specify how many lines of space you want between the lines of text

⑥ Use the arrows or type a value. For the Exactly and At Least settings, this is a distance measurement, usually in points; for Multiple, this is the number of lines of space. Click OK.

> **Tip**
> The default measure for spacing is the *point*, abbreviated as "pt." A point is a typographic measure: 72 points equal 1 inch (28.57 points equal 1 centimeter).

> **Tip**
> Press Ctrl+1 for single spacing, Ctrl+5 for 1.5 line spacing, Ctrl+2 for double spacing, and Ctrl+0 (zero) for one line before the paragraph. Ctrl+0 is a toggle, so you can use it to change a paragraph from one line before to no lines before.

Set the Line Spacing Between Paragraphs

1 Click in a paragraph or select the paragraphs you want to change, and then click the Line Spacing tool in the Home tab.

2 Click the command for adding space before or after the paragraph or paragraphs.

3 If you want to customize the spacing, click Line Spacing Options to display the Paragraph dialog box.

4 In the Before and After boxes, use the arrows or type a value for the space before (above) the first line of the paragraph and for the space after (below) the last line of the paragraph.

5 Select this check box if you don't want space between paragraphs of the same style.

6 Click OK.

7 If you want to remove the space before or after the selected paragraph or paragraphs, click the Line Spacing tool again, and choose Remove Space Before Paragraph or Remove Space After Paragraph from the menu.

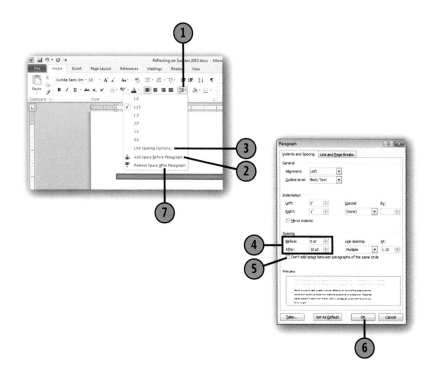

Caution

Note that the distance between two paragraphs is the sum of the space below the first paragraph and the space above the second paragraph. Keep this in mind so that you don't end up with a bigger space between paragraphs than you intended.

Adjusting the Spacing Between Characters

Sometimes you'll need to squeeze a little more text onto a line; at other times you'll want to spread the text out to fill up a line. Perhaps you want to create a special look in a heading by condensing or expanding the text. You can achieve all these effects by adjusting the widths of characters and the spaces between characters and between words.

Adjust the Spacing

① Select the text whose spacing you want to adjust.

② On the Home tab, click the Font tool to display the Font dialog box and click the Advanced tab.

③ Change the settings to adjust the spacing:

- In the Scale box, click a percentage in the list, or type the percentage by which you want to expand or condense the width of each character.

- In the Spacing box, click Expanded or Condensed in the list; in the By text box, enter a value to expand or condense the spacing between characters.

④ To *kern*—that is, to decrease the spacing between—certain pairs of letters, select this check box and specify a minimum font size to be kerned. (Word uses its own list to determine which letter pairs, in which fonts, can be kerned.)

⑤ Click OK.

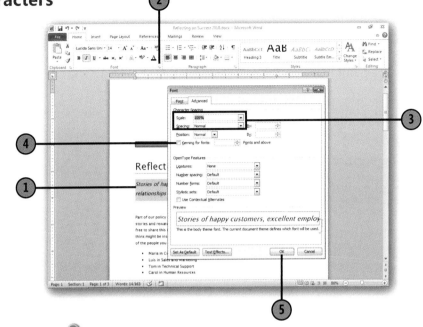

Caution

As a side effect of increasing or decreasing the character spacing, Word also adjusts the spacing between words.

See Also

"Add WordArt Elements" on page 148 for information about adjusting the character spacing in WordArt.

Tip

Also in the Advanced tab you'll find the OpenType settings, which enable you to use Word 2010's high-end typography features that are available with some OpenType fonts. Now for the fonts that support it (such as Gabriola, which comes with Word 2010), you can set ligatures, stylistic sets, and number styles, which give you additional ways to format and display the text.

Setting Paragraph Alignment

Choosing the alignment of the paragraphs in your document plays an important part in drawing the reader's eye down the page. You can experiment with different alignments to get just the right look, but in most cases you won't want to stray too far from the traditional left alignment. For some special elements, such as quotes, headings, or captions, you may want to liven things up with centered or right alignment.

Set the Alignment

(1) Click in a paragraph or select the paragraphs you want to change.

(2) In the Paragraph group of the Home tab, click one of the following:

- Align Left to align the paragraph with the left margin or left indent. Align Left creates a ragged right margin.

- Center to center the text between the margins or between the indents, if those settings are used.

- Align Right to align the paragraph with the right margin or right indent. Align Right creates a ragged left margin.

- Justify to align the paragraph with both margins or with both indents (if used). Justify adds space between words to align both the left and right margins or indents.

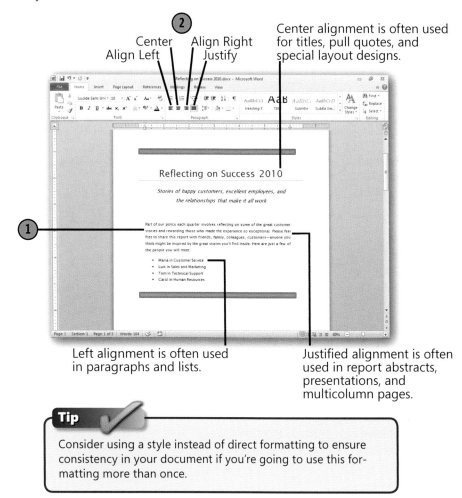

Center alignment is often used for titles, pull quotes, and special layout designs.

Left alignment is often used in paragraphs and lists.

Justified alignment is often used in report abstracts, presentations, and multicolumn pages.

Tip Consider using a style instead of direct formatting to ensure consistency in your document if you're going to use this formatting more than once.

Indenting a Paragraph

When you want to set a paragraph off from other paragraphs and change the amount of space between the margin and the text, consider using an indent. The indent can be as simple as slightly indenting the first line to indicate the start of a new paragraph, or as complex as indenting both the left and right edges of the paragraph to create a separate block of text.

Indent a Paragraph

1. Click in a paragraph or select the paragraphs you want to change.

2. Click the dialog launcher in the Paragraph group on the Home tab.

3. Click in the Left box and use the arrows, or type a value for the distance you want the indent from the left margin.

4. Click in the Right box and set the distance for the indent from the right margin.

5. Select this check box if you want the left and right indents to switch depending on whether they're on odd or even pages.

6. Click in the Special box, and select one of the following:

   • First Line to indent the first line

   • Hanging to indent all the lines in the paragraph except the first line

7. Click in the By box and use the arrows, or type a value for the size you want the indent to be.

8. Click OK.

First Line Indent Marker
Left Indent Marker
Right Indent Marker

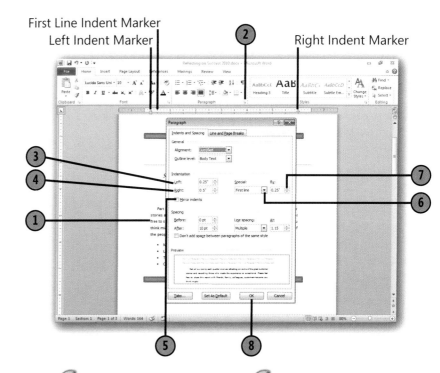

Tip
The Mirror Indents option is designed for two-sided documents, so you'll notice that the Left label changes to Inside and the Right label changes to Outside.

Tip
Using the ruler, you can easily set the indents by dragging the Left Indent, First Line Indent, and Right Indent markers. You can also create a left indent in a paragraph by clicking the Home tab and then clicking the Increase Indent tool. When you set indents using the Paragraph dialog box, however, you can specify precise values for all the indents.

Formatting with Tabs

Tabs give some people fits, but they are actually easy to work with in Word 2010. There are already tabs set by default every half-inch across the width of your document. You can use these tabs to position text horizontally on a line simply by pressing the Tab key. You can also set your own tabs and customize their effects by choosing different types of leaders—dotted, dashed, or plain lines—that appear before the tab stop.

Set Your Tabs

① Click the View tab and click the Ruler check box to display the ruler.

② Click the paragraph or select all paragraphs where you want to set the tabs.

③ Click to select the type of tab you want. Each click selects a different type of tab or other ruler marker.

④ Click in the ruler where you want the tabs. If necessary, drag a tab stop to a new location to adjust it.

⑤ Repeat steps 3 and 4 to set additional tab stops.

⑥ Drag a tab stop off the ruler to delete that tab stop.

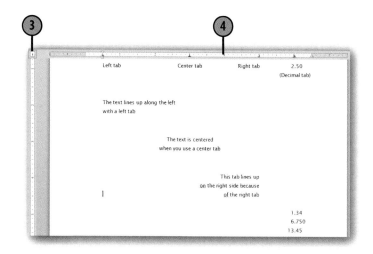

Tip ✓
Consider using a table instead of tab stops when you want to align several lines of text into columns.

See Also
"Creating a Table from Scratch" on page 111 for information about setting tabs in table cells.

Modify the Tabs

1. Double-click any tab stop on the ruler to display the Tabs dialog box.

2. Select the tab stop you want to modify.

3. Select an alignment for the tab stop.

4. Select a leader for the tab stop.

5. Click Set.

6. Do any of the following:

   • Set a new value for the default tab stops.

   • Specify a position for a new tab stop, set its alignment and leader, and click Set.

   • Select an existing tab stop, and click Clear to delete it.

   • Clear all tab stops.

7. Click OK.

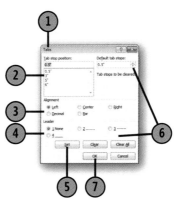

 Tip

You can also display the Tabs dialog box by clicking the Home tab, clicking the Paragraph dialog launcher, and then clicking the Tabs button in the Paragraph dialog box.

Tip

If the Page Setup dialog box appears instead of the Tabs dialog box, you clicked an inactive part of the ruler instead of a tab stop. Try again!

Adding Text Boxes

For special effects in the formatting of your page, you may want to add elements such as sidebars and pull quotes. Sidebars are often used to provide information that is related to—but not directly part of—the main text. Pull quotes can call attention to important thoughts used within the body text. Both can add a professional look to your page and help readers remember what's most important about the information you're presenting. Word provides a variety of predesigned text boxes you can use for sidebars and pull quotes, and you can also create and save your own text boxes for use in your documents.

Insert a Predesigned Text Box

1. Switch to Print Layout view if necessary.

2. In the Text group of the Insert tab, click the Text Box tool. In the gallery that appears, click the text box design you like.

(continued on next page)

Tip

If you'd rather draw your own text box instead of using one from the Text Box gallery, click Text Box and choose Draw Text Box. You can now add your own text and format the box as you'd like, using the tools on the Drawing Tools Format tab.

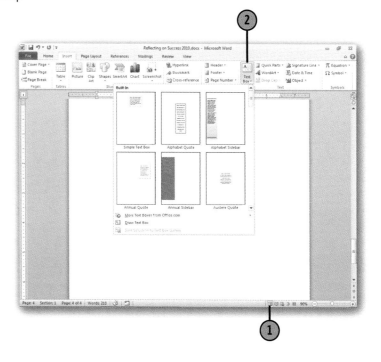

Insert a Predesigned Text Box *(continued)*

(3) Select any sample text in the text box, and paste or type your replacement text.

(4) Click the outer boundary of the text box and drag it to the location you want.

(5) Choose tools on the Drawing Tools Format tab to modify the text box itself or use the formatting tools on the Home tab to modify the text.

(6) Click outside the text box to resume working on the main content of your document.

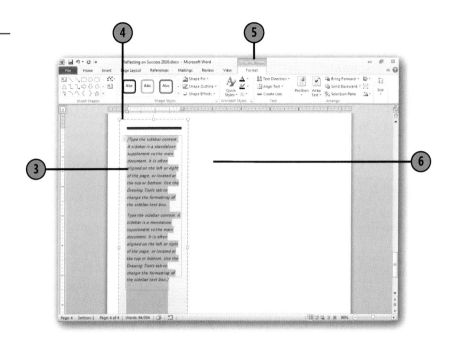

Link Text Box Text

(1) Create, format, and position the text boxes as you want them.

(2) Click the first text box to select it, and type or paste the text you want.

(3) On the Text Box Tools Format tab, click the Create Link tool.

(4) Click inside the text box into which you want to flow the text.

(5) Add line breaks or blank paragraphs to control the way the text flows from one text box to another.

(6) Adjust the size and position of each text box if necessary.

(7) If you want to link additional text boxes, select the last linked box and repeat steps 3 and 4.

See Also

"Adding Shapes" on page 135 for information about using a text box with a shape to create special effects with your text.

Tip

To select all the text in all the linked text boxes, click in one of the boxes and press Ctrl+A.

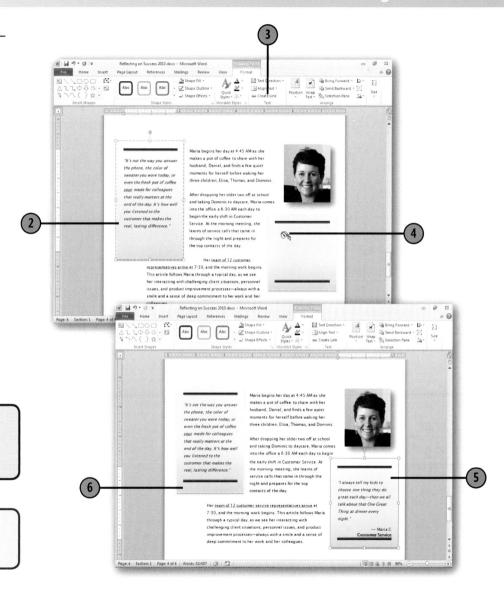

Creating a Dropped Capital Letter

If you want to create a special effect at the opening of a chapter or section in your document, you can add a *drop cap* to your text. A drop cap, which is a short way to say "dropped capital," simply changes the format of the opening character so that it adds a graphic element to the introduction of your text.

Create a Drop Cap

1. Click to the right of the first letter of your paragraph.

2. Click the Insert tab and click Drop Cap in the Text group.

3. Preview the different styles and click the one you want to apply.

4. If you don't see a style you like or want to customize the settings, click Drop Cap Options.

5. Do any of the following to customize the drop cap:

   - Specify a different font.

   - Specify a different number of lines over which you want the drop cap to extend.

   - Specify an increased or decreased horizontal distance between the drop cap and the text.

6. Click OK.

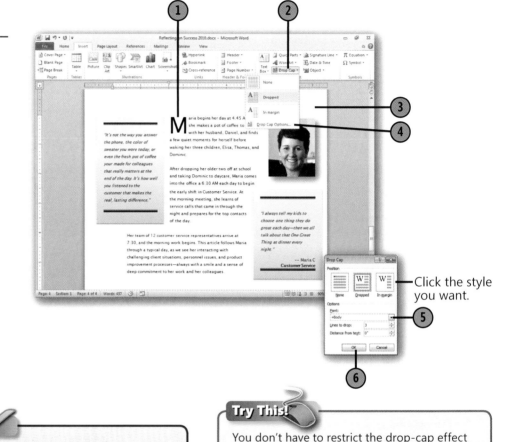

Click the style you want.

Tip

A drop cap is created as a separate paragraph, using a frame, so you can add borders and shading to it as you can to any paragraph.

Try This!

You don't have to restrict the drop-cap effect to one solitary letter. Try selecting several letters, or even an entire word, and then apply a drop cap.

Copying Your Formatting

If you want to apply formatting to multiple items in your document, you can use the Format Painter tool to select the formatting, copy it, and apply it to other items. This feature is great for those times when you create a special format that isn't a part of a style but that you want to apply to headings or quote text throughout a document.

Copy a Character Format

① Click the Home tab and then click the Show/Hide ¶ tool in the Paragraph group to display paragraph marks.

② Select the text with the formatting you want to copy. If you want to copy paragraph formatting, make sure your selection includes the paragraph mark at the end of the paragraph.

③ On the Home tab, click the Format Painter tool in the Clipboard group.

④ Drag the Format Painter over the selected text to apply the formatting and then release the button.

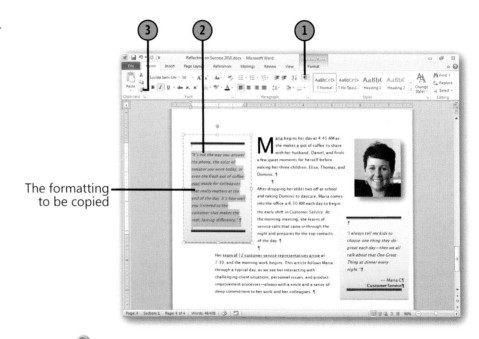

The formatting to be copied

Tip

To copy formatting to several locations, double-click the Format Painter tool after you've selected your text. You can now copy the formatting to as many places as you want. When you've finished, press the Esc key or click the Format Painter again.

Caution

You can't copy multiple types of formatting at one time. For example, in a selection in which the first word is formatted in bold and the next word is in italics, only the bold formatting will be applied when you use the Format Painter.

Tip

To copy only paragraph formatting, select only the paragraph mark before you click the Format Painter tool.

Placing a Line Border Around a Page

Depending on the overall design of your document, you may want to add a border around the page. Word 2010 includes a number of line styles you can use to add and customize the borders you add.

Create a Page Border

1. Click the View tab and click the One Page tool in the Zoom group to display one entire page of your document.

2. Click the Page Layout tab, click Page Borders, and, in the Borders And Shading dialog box that appears, click the Page Border tab.

3. Click the type of border you want.

4. Specify a line style, color, and width.

5. To remove an existing border from one side of the page, click the border that represents the side of the page whose border you want to remove. To add a border, click a border that represents a side of the page that doesn't have a border.

6. Specify the part of the document that you want to have this border.

7. Click Options to change the distance of the border from the edge of the page or the text, and to specify whether you want the running heads to be surrounded by this border.

8. Click OK.

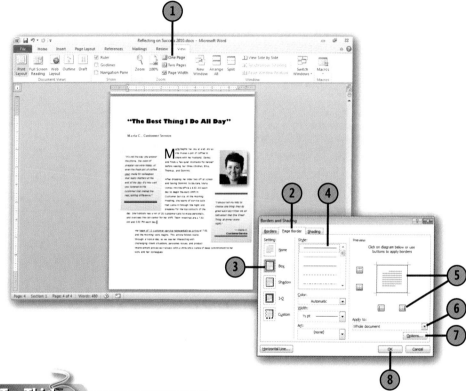

Try This!

Insert a page border. Click a button to remove the border from one side. Specify a different line style, width, or color; and click the same border button. Repeat to modify the other sides to create a custom border.

See Also

"Adding a Border or Shading to a Paragraph" on page 95 for information about placing a border around a paragraph.

Placing an Art Border Around a Page

If you want to be a little more dramatic with your page border, you can add one with artistic embellishments. Word 2010 includes a number of special art borders that enable you to border your pages with ice cream cones, flowers, ladybugs, and more. This offers a fun design touch for party invitations, brochures, flyers, and more.

Create an Art Border

1 Click the View tab and click One Page in the Zoom group.

2 Click the Page Layout tab, click Page Borders in the Page Background group, and click the Page Border tab of the Borders And Shading dialog box.

3 Click the Box setting.

4 Choose the art style you want to use for your border.

5 Specify the width you want for the border art; if the Color list is available, choose the color you want.

6 Click a border to remove it. To replace the border, click the border's button.

7 Specify the part of the document that you want to have the selected border.

8 Click Options if you want to change the distance of the border from the page edge or from the text.

9 Click OK.

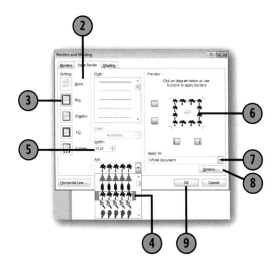

Tip Unlike the way you can mix and match line borders, you can use only one type of art border for all the sides of the page.

Adding a Decorative Horizontal Line

A horizontal line can be more than just a line. In Word it can be a curvy, colorful line or picture, or it can be as simple as a series of dots and dashes. Whichever style of horizontal line you choose, you can customize it in a way that fits your document's design.

Add a Line

1. Click at the point in your document where you want the horizontal line to appear.

2. Click the Page Layout tab, click the Page Borders tool of the Page Background group, and click the Horizontal Line button in the Borders And Shading dialog box.

3. Click the horizontal line style you want to use.

4. Click OK.

5. Double-click the line to display the Format Horizontal Line dialog box. Make any modifications you want to the line.

6. On the Picture tab, make any further adjustments.

7. Click OK.

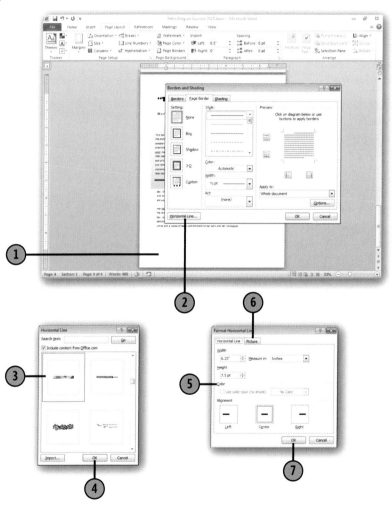

Adding a Border or Shading to a Paragraph

You can set off special paragraphs, text sections, sidebars, and more by adding a border or shading to a paragraph. This enables you to call attention to specific information on the page.

Add a Border

(1) Click in the paragraph you want to border.

(2) Click the Page Layout tab, click Page Borders, and click the Borders tab of the Borders And Shading dialog box.

(3) Click the type of border you want.

(4) Specify a line style, color, and width.

(5) Click a border if you want to remove the border from one or more sides of the paragraph. To replace the border, click the button again.

(6) Specify Paragraph.

(7) Click Options if you want to change the distance of the border from the text. Click OK.

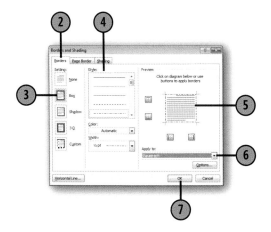

Add Shading

1. Click the Page Layout tab, click Page Borders, and, in the Borders And Shading dialog box, click the Shading tab.

2. Click the color you want.

3. If you want to add a pattern, click the Style arrow and choose the percentage of color that will show in the paragraph.

4. Choose Paragraph.

5. Click OK.

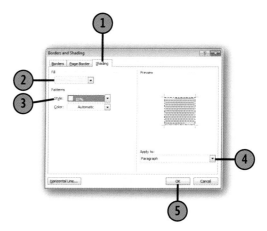

Try This!

Select a word or a sentence, but don't select a whole paragraph. Open the Borders And Shading dialog box, add a border and some shading, and, in the Apply To box, specify Text. Click OK.

5

Designing Great Layouts

Not every page you create in Microsoft Word 2010 will need careful thought about the layout of the page. You might whip off a quick memo to a co-worker, for example, that doesn't require anything special about the way the text appears on the page. But some documents—such as annual reports, newsletters, sales brochures, and training booklets—require a little more thought. And if you expect to be using the design again and again, all the better—extra thought about the layout of the document now can save you time and trouble later.

Your layout is a lot like the "bones" of your document—the beneath-the-surface underpinning that gives the finished work its sense of balance and structure. As you work through this section of the book, whether you're actually putting your layout together now or just getting ideas for an upcoming project, you'll see that Word 2010 gives you many different ways—and a number of powerful tools—to make creating effective layouts simple and straightforward.

Customizing a Template

Word 2010 includes a number of professionally designed templates with your version of the program, and what's more, when you click the File tab and click New, you have the benefit of browsing dozens and dozens of additional templates available from Office.com. No matter what color, font, style, or design you want, chances are that you'll find a template that comes close. No matter how well designed, however, no template can be everything to all people, and it's likely that you'll want to do some customizing to make the template fit your particular project.

Open the Template

1. Click the File tab and click New.

2. Click My Templates.

3. Click the template you want to modify.

4. Click Template in the Create New section.

5. Click OK.

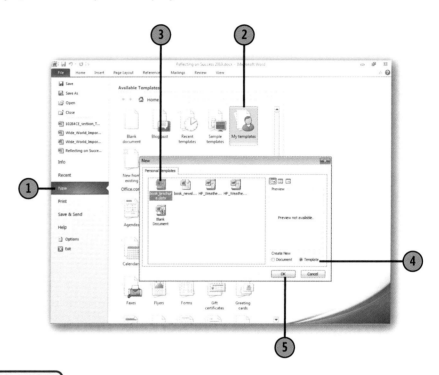

Tip

If you want to make changes to a template that's either stored on a company Web site or available from Office.com, you won't be able to open the template as a template. Instead, you'll need to open it as a document, make your modifications, and then save the document as a template on your computer.

See Also

"Designing a Template" on page 100 for information about designing your own template.

Modify the Template

① Click Save on the Quick Access Tool-bar, type a unique and descriptive file name for your new template, and click Save.

② On the Home tab, click the Show/Hide ¶ tool in the Paragraph group to display paragraph marks.

③ Replace the placeholder text with any text you want to include as part of the template.

④ Add any new text or other page elements.

⑤ Redefine or create your own para-graph styles and character styles.

⑥ Click File and save and close the template.

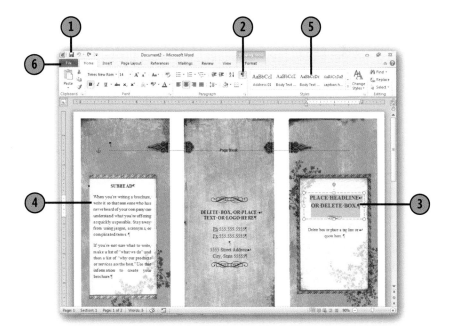

Tip

The modified template will be saved in your personal Tem-plates folder and will appear in the New dialog box when you choose New in Backstage view and click My Templates.

Try This!

Click File, click New, click My Templates, and create a document based on the modified template to verify that the template is correct.

See Also

"Creating a Template from Scratch" on page 101 for informa-tion about starting a document based on a template.

Designing a Template

You may find that none of the available templates is exactly what you need for your project, so you decide to create a template from scratch. The easiest way to do this is to use an existing document and set it up as a template. If you don't have an existing document that incorporates all the special elements you need, create one and then save it. Review the entire document to determine whether the design really works and then close the document. You'll be using a copy of the document as the basis for your template's design, so if you don't like the resulting template, you can simply delete it and then revise it using the same document.

Base Your Template Design on an Existing File

1. Click File and choose New.

2. Click New From Existing; in the New From Existing Document dialog box, navigate to the document you want to use and click Open.

3. Click File and click Save As, and click the Templates folder.

4. Type a unique and descriptive file name.

5. Verify that Word Template is shown in the Save As Type list.

6. Select this check box to save a thumbnail image of the template.

7. Click Save.

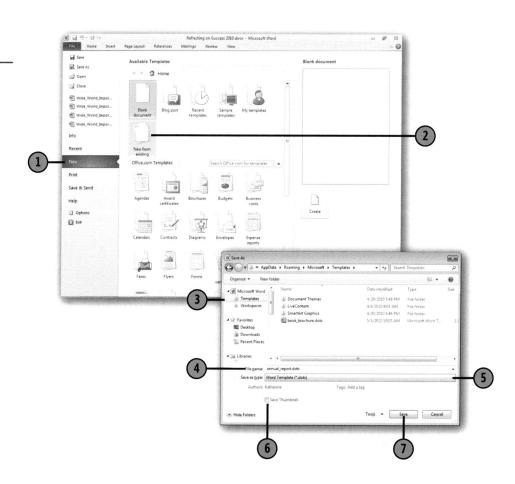

Create a Template from Scratch

(1) On the Home tab, click Show/Hide ¶ in the Paragraph group if necessary.

(2) Add any text you want to appear in all documents based on this template.

(3) Add your logo, header information, or tagline.

(4) Add fields for mail merge or content collection.

(5) Add hyperlinks you want to include.

(6) Click Save in the Quick Access Toolbar to save the template.

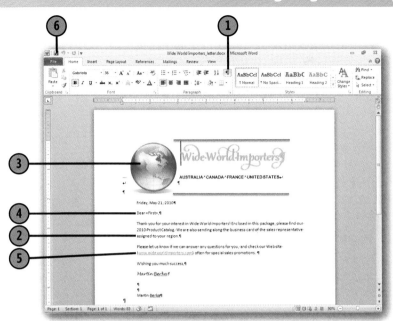

To include the date and time in the template and to have Word update both each time you create a new document, click the Date & Time tool on the Insert tab in the Text group, click the format you want to use, select the Update Automatically check box, and click OK.

So what are fields, anyway? Word 2010 fields, also called *content controls*, enable you to include placeholders for information in your document that might change. For example, the Date & Time tool in the Text group of the Insert tab inserts a field that will update with the current date and time.

To locate the fields in your template while you're designing it, or to see the fields in documents based on the template so that you don't accidentally delete them, click File and click Options. Click Advanced, and, in the Show Document Content section, specify whether you want fields to be shaded when they're selected or always to be shaded. Click OK to close the Word Options dialog box.

In addition to repeating text, fields, columns, and perhaps a logo or headline you want to include in your template, you can also include building blocks (perhaps your mission statement), AutoText, and even macros you want to be available in the documents created based on that template.

Laying Out the Page

Just a few years ago, the printer was the likely destination for any document you created. Today you may share a document electronically, post it as a blog, send it to a Windows Live account, or e-mail it to team members. When you do plan to print a document, you have additional items to consider for your layout. Will you print the page in landscape or portrait orientation? Will the document be printed on both sides of the page? Thinking through these types of issues as you design your page helps you ensure that you get just the kind of print-out you were expecting.

Set Up a Standard Page

1 Click the Page Layout tab, click Size in the Page Setup group, and click the page size you want.

2 If you don't see the page size you want, click More Paper Sizes.

3 Choose your paper size on the Paper tab of the Page Setup dialog box.

4 Click the Margins tab and select the margins settings you want.

5 Click Orientation, and select the orientation: Portrait (longer than wide) or Landscape (wider than long).

6 Click OK.

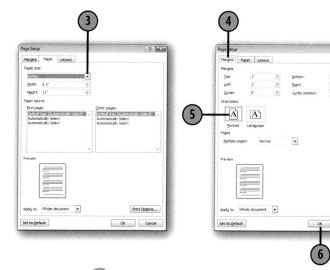

See Also

"Creating Variable Running Heads" on page 178 for information about using different headers and footers in a two-sided document.

Tip

You can also set document margins and change orientation by clicking tools in the Page Setup group of the Page Layout tab.

Tip

The gutter is the extra space you add to the margin where the document is to be bound so that the text won't be hidden by the binding.

Set Up a Two-Sided Document

1 Click the Page Layout tab, click Margins in the Page Setup group, and choose Custom Margins.

2 Click the Margins tab, and click Mirror Margins in the Multiple Pages list.

3 Set the document's side margins using the Inside and Outside boxes. The Inside margin will be on the left side of odd-numbered (right-hand, or *recto*) pages and on the right side of even-numbered (left-hand, or *verso*) pages.

4 Click OK.

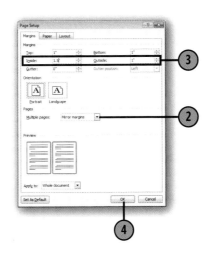

Tip

You can apply a gutter to any document layout. For a document that's set up for one-sided printing, you can specify the gutter location as the left side of the paper or the top of the paper. For a multiple-page layout, Word uses the default location of the gutter for the type of layout you choose. Use the preview to see the placement of the gutter.

Set Up a Bound Document

1 Click Margins and choose Custom Margins.

2 Click the Margins tab and specify a value for the gutter.

3 If the Multiple Pages list is set to Normal, specify whether the gutter (and therefore the binding) should be on the left side or at the top of the page. For other Multiple Pages settings, the gutter position is set automatically.

4 Click OK.

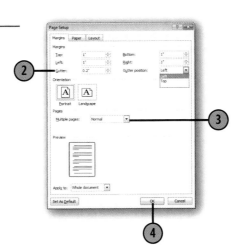

Changing Page Orientation

Different parts of a long document sometimes require different layouts. For example, although most of your document's text may be in portrait orientation, there might be one or two pages you want to include with tables, figures, or other special elements that need to be set up in landscape mode because of their width. By dividing the document into sections, you can set up each section with its own orientation.

Change the Page Orientation

1. Select the part of the document whose page orientation you want to change.

2. Click the Page Layout tab, click Margins in the Page Setup group, and choose Custom Margins.

3. Click the orientation you want.

4. In the Apply To list, choose Selected Text.

5. Click OK.

6. Use the Zoom Control on the status bar to see your pages in detail, and verify that the layout is what you want.

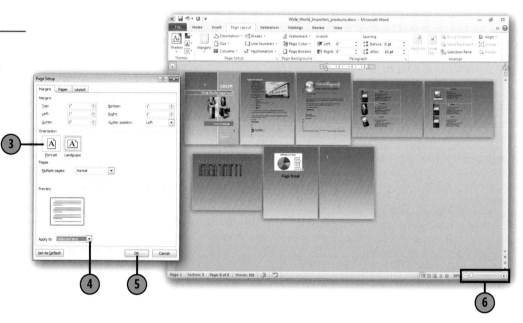

Tip

When you change the orientation of selected text, you're actually creating two new sections: one for the selected text and another for the text that follows the selection.

Tip

If you click the Show/Hide tool in the Paragraph group of the Home tab, you will see that Word 2010 added a section break at the beginning and end of the section you just set to landscape orientation.

Tip

If you want to change the orientation of the document from the current point forward, you can use the Orientation tool in the Page Setup group of the Page Layout tab to make the change.

Changing Margins in a Document

Most of your documents may require only one set of margins, and you use paragraph indents to control the layout of individual paragraphs. Sometimes, though, a long document might have several large sections that need different margins. Setting different margins for different sections would be extremely time-consuming and tedious to do when using paragraph indents. Instead, you can set each section to start on a new page or even to start on the same page as a section that has different margins.

Change the Margins

1. Select the part of the document whose margins you want to change.

2. On the Page Layout tab, click Margins in the Page Setup group, and click Custom Margins.

3. Set the new margins.

4. Specify Selected Text.

5. Click the Layout tab, and specify the point at which the section with the changed margins will start. Specify Continuous if you want the changed section to begin on the same page as the previous section.

6. Click OK.

7. Click in the next section of your document, and redisplay the Layout tab. Specify where you want this section to start. Click OK.

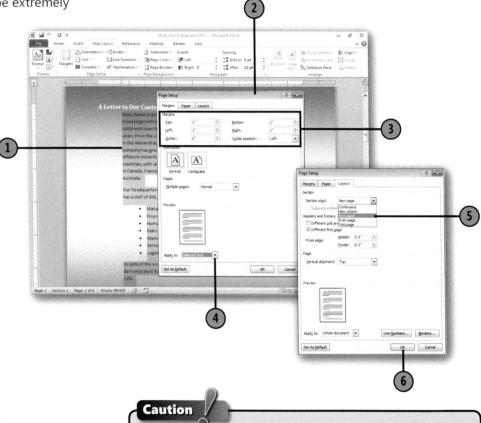

See Also

"Adding Columns" on page 110 for information about using a multiple-column layout.

Caution

Click Show/Hide in the Paragraph group to see the section markers that have been added. Don't delete the markers or else you'll lose your new margin settings.

Fine-Tuning Your Layout

One of the great things about creating documents in Word 2010 is that you never need to be completely done with a document—unless you choose to, that is. You can turn a report into a letter, a letter into a brochure, a brochure into postcards, and so on. Electronic documents means never having to say you're finished! After you've chosen the new layout for the text, you may need to adjust the flow by changing the way the lines break or adjusting the paragraphs. Here's how to do that.

Adjust Text Flow

(1) Select the paragraph or paragraphs in which you want to make changes.

(2) On the Home tab, click the dialog launcher in the Paragraph group.

(3) Click the Line And Page Breaks tab.

(4) Select or clear this check box to control the way paragraphs break across consecutive pages.

(5) Select this check box if the paragraph is a heading that must always be on the same page as the beginning of the following paragraph.

(6) Select this check box if you never want to allow a paragraph to break across pages.

(7) Click OK.

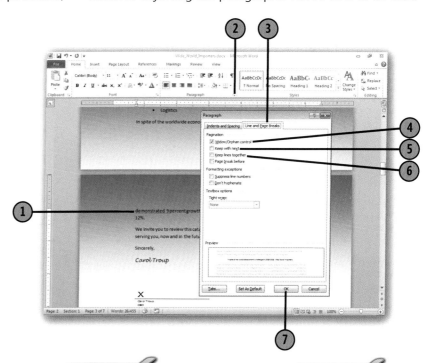

Tip ✓

There are many definitions of the terms *widow* and *orphan* in the publishing world. In Word's world, widows and orphans are single lines that get separated from the paragraph to which they belong and become marooned alone at the top (orphan) or bottom (widow) of a page. Widows and orphans are considered aesthetically undesirable in both worlds.

Tip ✓

Breaking manually means that when you don't like the place where Word automatically ended, or broke, a line (or a word, a column, or a page, for that matter), you can change the break yourself.

Tip ✓

To change widow and orphan control throughout a document, change the setting for the paragraph format in the style definition.

Adjust Hyphenation

1 Click Hyphenation in the Page Setup group of the Page Layout tab.

2 Click the hyphenation setting you want to apply to the document.

3 To fine-tune hyphenation settings, click Hyphenation Options.

4 Click to have Word automatically hyphenate your document.

5 Set the amount of space from the right text margin where you want words to be hyphenated.

6 Choose whether you want to limit the number of hyphenations that appear in a row.

7 Click OK.

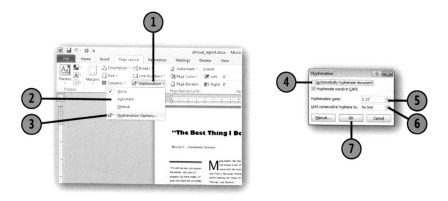

Caution

Always apply manual page breaks as the very last adjustment you make to a document before you print it. Editing a document after you've applied page breaks can result in an unacceptably short page or an extra blank page. However, if you do need to edit the document after page breaking, click File and click Print to preview your document and examine the page breaks.

Tip

When you adjust the line breaks manually, try to get the resulting right-hand paragraph edges into the shape of a backward letter "C"—that is, try to make the first and last lines of the paragraph shorter than the other lines.

Creating Sections

When you are working with really long documents, you'll find it easier to control headers and footers, page numbers, and more if you divide the document into sections. Word will start your chapters or sections on odd-numbered pages and will create running heads to your specifications.

Start a New Section

① Click where you want to begin the new section.

② Click Breaks in the Page Setup group of the Page Layout tab. Click Odd Page. Word inserts the section break in front of the insertion point.

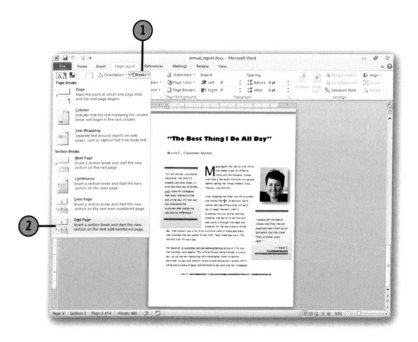

Change the Running Heads

① Click the Insert tab, click the Header tool in the Header & Footer group, and click Edit Header. Any text in the header comes from the previous header.

② On the Header & Footer Tools Design tab, click the Link To Previous tool to turn it off and to disconnect the header from the previous header.

③ Replace the old header text, if any, with the text for your new running head.

④ Click the Go To Footer tool to move to the footer, and repeat steps 2 and 3 for the footer. If the document is set for a different running head on the first page, or for different running heads on odd- and even-numbered pages, repeat steps 2 and 3 for those running heads.

⑤ Click Close Header And Footer when you've finished.

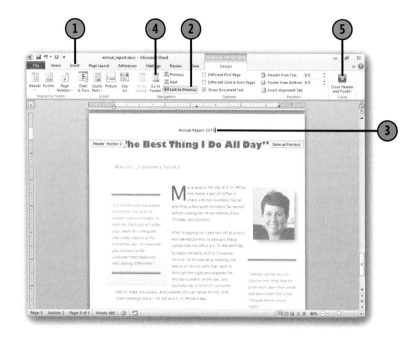

Tip

When you use an Odd Page section break to start a new chapter, note that if the previous section of your document ended on an odd-numbered page, Word will insert a blank even-numbered page so that your chapter will start on the odd-numbered page.

Adding Columns

Columns add special layout style to documents that contain a lot of text. You might add columns in a newsletter, a brochure, or sales literature. Word 2010 makes it easy for you to flow text into columns on your page. You can set up multiple columns, change the width of columns, and even add divider lines to help add more visual interest to the page.

Change the Number of Columns

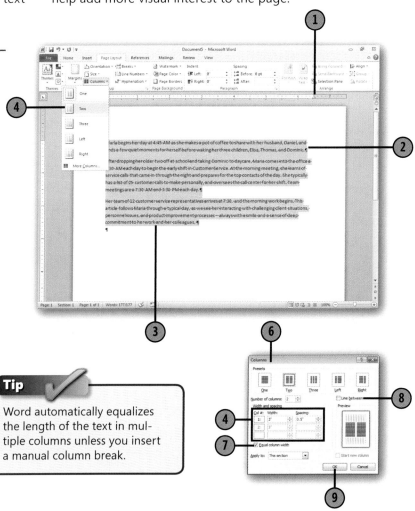

1. Without worrying about the layout just yet, complete the content of your document. Make sure the page orientation and the margins are set correctly for the document.

2. On the Home tab, click the Show/Hide ¶ tool in the Paragraph group if it isn't already turned on.

3. Select the text that you want to flow into columns.

4. On the Page Layout tab, click Columns in the Page Setup group, and select the layout you want. Word makes the selected text into a separate section by inserting Continuous section breaks before and after the selected text.

5. If you want to adjust the columns, click anywhere in the section that has the columns.

6. Click the Columns tool again, and click More Columns in the Columns gallery to display the Columns dialog box.

7. If you don't want even-width columns, clear this check box, and then specify the width you want for each column.

8. Select this check box if you want a vertical line centered between adjacent columns.

9. Make sure the settings are applied only to the selected text, and then click OK.

Tip

Word automatically equalizes the length of the text in multiple columns unless you insert a manual column break.

Creating a Table from Scratch

Tables are your friends. They give you a simple, logical way to align numbers, text, and pictures on your page. Word 2010 offers a number of ways you can create a table, but the simplest and most versatile method is to create an empty, unformatted table with a prescribed number of rows and columns. You can easily add content, and you can format and modify it later.

Create a Table

① Click the Insert tab and click the Table tool. Move the mouse pointer to select the number of rows and columns you want in your table, and then click to insert the table.

② Click in the first cell and insert your content.

③ Press Tab to move to the next cell, and add your content. (Press Enter only to start a new paragraph inside a table cell.) Continue pressing Tab and entering content to complete your table. If you've reached the end of your table but you still need to enter more items, press Tab, and Word creates a new row.

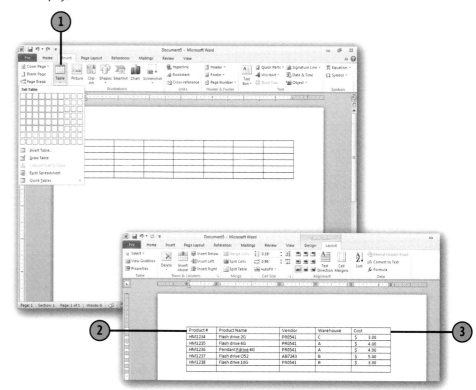

See Also

"Creating a Table from Text" on page 114 for information about converting existing text in paragraphs into text in a table.

Tip

To move to the previous cell, press Shift+Tab. To insert a tab inside a cell, press Ctrl+Tab.

The Anatomy of a Table

The Move box appears when the mouse pointer is positioned over the table in Print Layout and Web Layout views.

A table cell

A cell marker

The text can be horizontal or vertical.

Table cells are merged into a single cell.

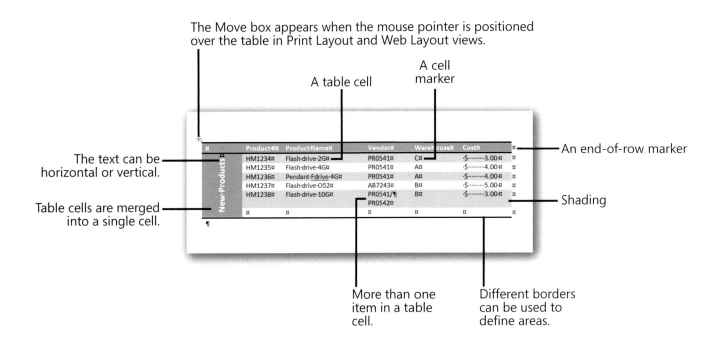

An end-of-row marker

Shading

More than one item in a table cell.

Different borders can be used to define areas.

Using a Predesigned Table

In the same way that you use templates for creating specialized types of documents, you can use a table template to create a specialized type of table, complete with formatting and related material—a title or caption, for example. The table designs you select are coordinated with the document theme you are using, so the colors, fonts, and effects will match the other items on your page.

Choose a Table

(1) Click in your document where you want the table to appear.

(2) On the Insert tab, click Table, point to Quick Tables, and click the type of table you want.

(3) Drag the mouse over the content of the table, and press the Delete key to remove the sample text.

(4) Click in the top-left cell, and type your information. Use the Tab key to move through the cells, and enter the rest of your content.

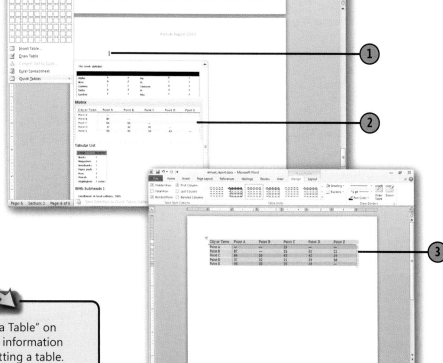

Tip

Once you've created the table, you can modify its appearance by applying table styles and other formatting.

See Also

"Formatting a Table" on page 124 for information about formatting a table.

Creating a Table from Text

It's possible to use tabs to align content in columns, but aligning your content means that the content can get seriously messed up if you decide to reformat the document with different fonts, margins, and layouts. One way to avoid this is to convert your text into a table. That way, not only is the formatting much simpler, but you can use the table tools to organize your information more easily.

Convert the Text

1. Make sure the content is correctly separated by tabs, commas, paragraphs, or other marks. Delete any extra tabs (more than one tab between columns, for example) even if this affects the current alignment.

2. Select all the text.

3. Click the Insert tab, click Table, and click Convert Text To Table.

4. Choose the number of columns you want to create.

5. Select the type of mark you used to separate the columns of text.

6. Click OK.

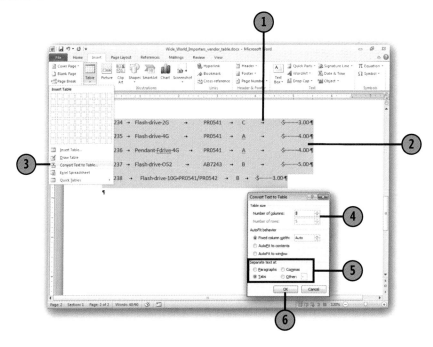

Adding or Deleting Rows and Columns in a Table

Of course, part of creating and working with a table means adding to it or removing bits you don't need. Word 2010 makes it easy for you to modify the layout of an existing table by adding or deleting rows and columns anywhere in the table.

Add Rows or Columns

1. Click in the table next to where you want to add a row or column.

2. On the Table Tools Layout tab, choose what you want to add.

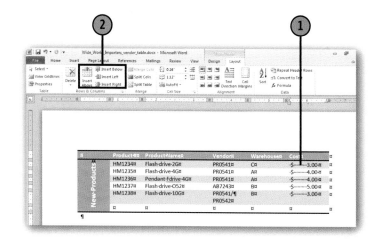

Tip

To delete the content of a row or column without deleting the row or column itself, select the row or column, and press the Delete key.

Caution

If you want to delete content from a row or column without deleting the row or column itself, make sure your selection doesn't extend outside the table. If it does, you'll delete whatever part of the table is selected as well as its content.

Try This!

Create a table with three columns and three rows. Click in the top-left cell. Drag the mouse to the right to select the first two cells. Click the Table Tools Layout tab and then click Insert Left. With the new columns selected, click Insert Above. Note that the number of rows and columns that are inserted is based on the number of rows and columns in which cells were selected. Now try deleting rows and columns to revert to the size of the original table.

Delete Rows or Columns

(1) Click in a table cell that's in the row or column you want to delete.

(2) On the Table Tools Layout tab, click Delete and choose what you want to delete.

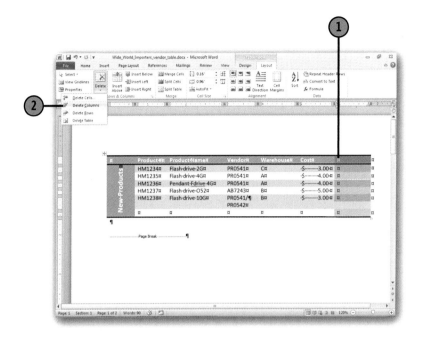

Positioning Elements in a Table

Getting things to line up is what a table is all about. You can use several special tools to align the text in your table. Not only can you center, left-align, or right-align the text in the table, but you also can actually change the text direction to create special effects for table row or column information.

Align the Text

① Create and format your table.

② Click in a cell or select all the cells to which you want to apply a specific alignment.

③ On the Table Tools Layout tab, click an Alignment tool to apply the alignment you want.

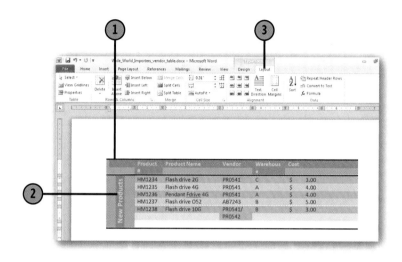

Try This!

Select an entire column in a table that will contain decimal numbers. Select the Decimal tab stop on the ruler, and click in the horizontal ruler to place the tab stop in the column. Your numbers will be aligned by their decimal points in that column.

See Also

"Customizing a Table Layout" on page 119 for information about changing the size of cells to accommodate sideways text.

See Also

"Formatting a Table" on page 124 for information about formatting a table.

Set the Text Direction

① Click in a cell or select all the cells to which you want to apply a specific text direction.

② On the Table Tools Layout tab, click the Text Direction tool. If the direction of the text isn't what you want, click the tool again.

③ Adjust the text alignment and the column and row dimensions as necessary.

To widen the cell for vertical text, click to increase this value.

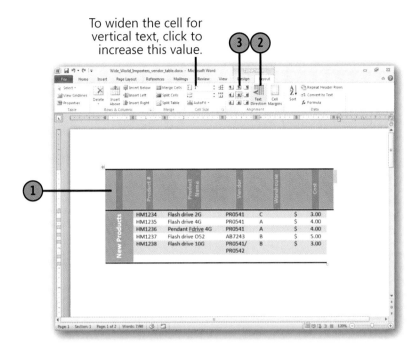

Customizing a Table Layout

Tailoring the table to fit and showcase your content in the best possible way is simple in Word 2010. You can change the width of columns or the height of rows, for example, or draw new cell boundaries and erase old ones. Word gives you a great deal of flexibility in the layout of your table.

Change the Table Size

1 In Print Layout view, move the mouse pointer over the table to make the Size box appear.

2 Drag the Size box to change the size of the table.

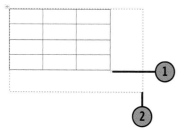

Tip ✔

To specify precise measurements for column width and row height, enter the values on the Table Tools Layout tab. To make all the cells the same height, click in a cell, and on the Table Tools Layout tab, click Distribute Rows.

Try This! 🖱

Make sure the ruler is displayed. Hold down the Alt key while you drag a cell boundary. Depending on whether you're dragging vertically or horizontally, the corresponding ruler shows the distance between the boundaries.

Change the Row or Column Size

① Move the mouse pointer over a vertical cell boundary until the pointer turns into a Move pointer. Drag the boundary left or right to change the size of the adjacent columns.

② Move the mouse pointer over a horizontal cell boundary, and drag the boundary up or down to change the height of the row.

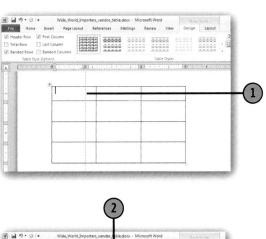

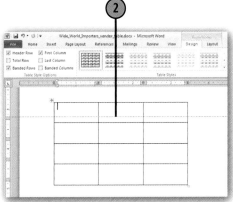

Divide One Cell into Two

1 Click in the table.

2 On the Table Tools Design tab, select the type of border, the border thickness, and the border color you want for the new boundary.

3 Click the Draw Table tool if it isn't already turned on. (You'll see a little pencil pointer on your screen when the tool is turned on.)

4 Drag the pencil pointer from a cell boundary to the opposite boundary. Add as many cell boundaries as you need. Click the Draw Table tool to turn it off when you've finished.

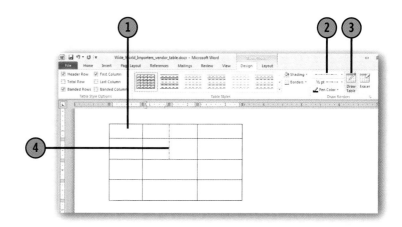

 Caution

When you're working on a table using the Draw Table and Eraser tools, it's difficult to achieve a high degree of precision. It's easy, for example, to accidentally add boundaries you don't want or delete those you do want. Carefully inspect your table after you add or delete a boundary. You can remedy an error by clicking the Undo tool on the Quick Access toolbar.

 Tip

You can also right-click the cell you want to split and choose Split Cells. If you want to combine more than one cell, select the cells, right-click your selection, and choose Merge Cells.

 Tip

If your table doesn't have borders and you can't see the cell boundaries, on the Table Tools Layout tab, click View Gridlines. These gridlines appear on the screen but won't be printed.

Aligning a Table

Ordinarily you'll want to position your table using the same alignment you choose for the surrounding text. However, you might want to set a table off a bit by changing its horizontal position—indenting or centering it, for example. By using Word's alignment settings instead of moving the table manually, you can ensure that the settings will remain in effect even if you change the margins or any other page settings.

Set the Alignment

1. Click the table, and then, on the Table Tools Layout tab, click the Properties tool in the Table group to display the Table Properties dialog box.

2. On the Table tab, click an alignment.

3. If you chose Left Alignment, specify the distance you want the table to be indented from the left margin.

4. If you want to the change the default alignment settings, click Around in the Text Wrapping section, click the Positioning button, make your changes in the Table Positioning dialog box that appears, and then click OK.

5. Click OK.

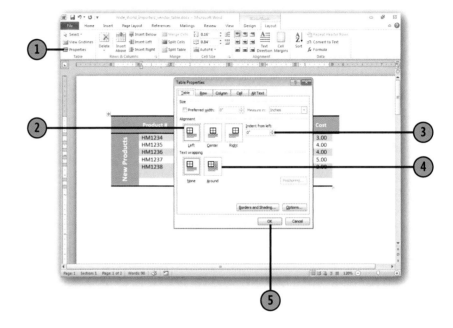

Try This!

Create two tables, one smaller than the other. Drag the smaller table and place it on top of the larger table. Note that the smaller table has become "nested" inside the larger table. Right-click in the nested table, choose Table Properties from the shortcut menu, and, on the Table tab of the Table Properties dialog box, click an alignment for the table. Click OK. Note that the alignment of the nested table is relative to the cell in which it's nested. Now click the Undo tool to return the tables to their original state.

See Also

"Moving a Table" on the facing page for information about setting text to wrap around a table.

Moving a Table

You can move a table just as you would move any object on your page—by clicking and dragging. You can also position a table precisely by using the tools available on the Table Tools Layout tab. When you drag a table, you can position it both horizontally and vertically on the page, just as you can position a picture on the page. When you move the table horizontally, you're also setting it to have text wrapping, so, if there's room, any text can wrap around all four sides of the table.

Move the Table

1. Switch to Print Layout view or Web Layout view if necessary by clicking the view tool in the lower-right corner of the screen.

2. Point to the table until the Move box appears.

3. Drag the Move box and the table to the location you want.

4. If you can't place the table in the exact location you want, or if the text isn't wrapping in the way you want, click Properties on the Table Tools Layout tab.

5. Specify the alignment relative to the text, and specify that you want the text to wrap around the table.

6. Click Positioning to display the Table Positioning dialog box.

7. Make any changes to the position of the table and specify how far the table should be from any surrounding text.

8. Click OK.

9. Click OK to close the Table Properties dialog box.

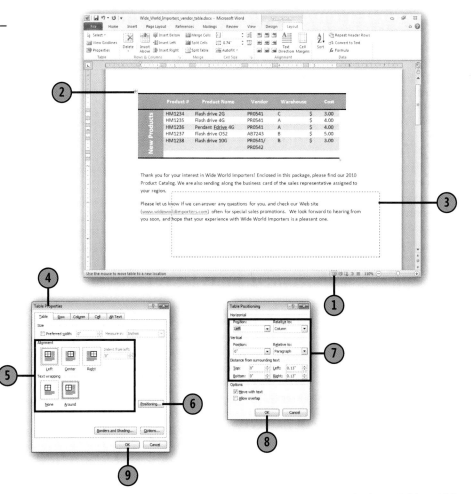

Formatting a Table

So you know how to use a table to organize your data—text, pictures, numbers, and more. Did you know you can also apply styles and formats to the table content you create? For example, you can use shading to delineate certain cell groupings, add borders to draw attention to particular cells, or use the formatting tools to vary the dimensions and alignment of the text.

Format a Table

1. Click inside the table.

2. On the Table Tools Design tab that appears, select a style for the table.

3. Select or clear the check boxes to turn the display of various table elements on or off, as desired.

4. Select the cell or cells to which you want to add or from which you want to remove shading, click the Shading tool and select a color to add shading, or select No Color to remove shading.

5. Select the cell or cells to which you want to add or from which you want to remove borders, click the Borders tool and select the borders you want, or select No Borders to remove the borders.

6. Click the Table Tools Layout tab, and use the tools to add or delete rows or columns, to set the dimensions of the rows and columns, and to set the text alignment, direction—that is, horizontal or vertical—and margins.

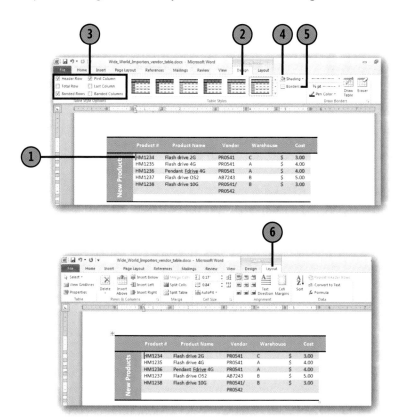

See Also

"Using a Predesigned Table" on page 113 for information about using a template to create a preformatted table.

Creating a Table Style

The styles you can apply to your tables in Word connect directly to the theme style you have selected or your document. Table styles in Word include special design elements including colors, shading, and more. You can use one of the table styles or modify one to best reflect what you'd like to see in your document. The easiest way to customize a table style is to create a table, apply an existing table style to it, and then modify the formatting to create your own style.

Create a Table Style

1 Create a table, and, on the Table Tools Design tab, apply the table style that's closest to what you have in mind.

2 Click the More button in the lower-right corner of the Table Styles group and click Modify Table Style.

3 Enter a new name for your style.

4 In Apply Formatting, click Whole Table in the drop-down list.

5 Use the formatting tools or click the Format button to specify any formatting that will be common to all the elements of the table—the font, for example. Click another element in the list, and use the formatting tools or click the Format button to redefine the formatting for that element. Continue clicking elements and changing their formatting as necessary.

6 Specify whether you want to have this style available in only this document or in all documents based on the current style.

7 Click OK.

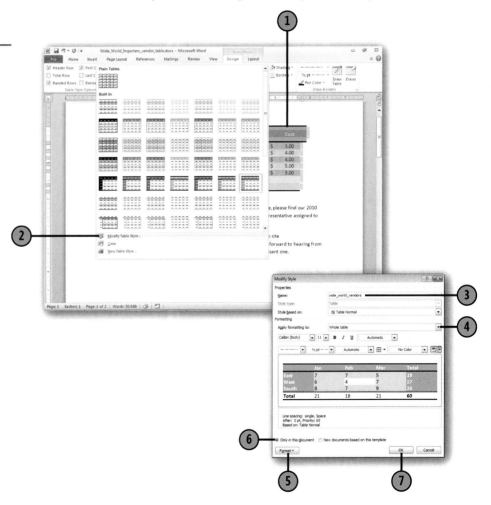

Add Shading

① Click the Page Layout tab, click Page Borders, and, in the Borders And Shading dialog box, click the Shading tab.

② Click the color you want.

③ If you want to add a pattern, click the Style arrow and choose the percentage of color that will show in the paragraph.

④ Choose Paragraph.

⑤ Click OK.

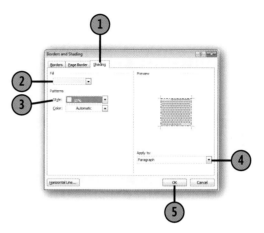

Try This!

Select a word or a sentence, but don't select a whole paragraph. Open the Borders And Shading dialog box, add a border and some shading, and, in the Apply To box, specify Text. Click OK.

Adding a Border or Shading to a Paragraph

You can set off special paragraphs, text sections, sidebars, and more by adding a border or shading to a paragraph. This enables you to call attention to specific information on the page.

Add a Border

1. Click in the paragraph you want to border.

2. Click the Page Layout tab, click Page Borders, and click the Borders tab of the Borders And Shading dialog box.

3. Click the type of border you want.

4. Specify a line style, color, and width.

5. Click a border if you want to remove the border from one or more sides of the paragraph. To replace the border, click the button again.

6. Specify Paragraph.

7. Click Options if you want to change the distance of the border from the text. Click OK.

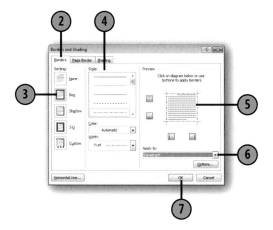

6

Adding Graphics to Your Documents

The images you add to your documents—whether you're creating a business report, a newsletter for your garden club, invitations for your son's graduation party, or a flyer for a new product—invite people in for a closer look. Images bring color, energy, and life to the words on the page. Whether you're showing pictures of happy people, capturing a beautiful landscape, spotlighting a product, or creating a piece of abstract art, the images in your document can inspire and uplift people, while encouraging them to stick around and read what you've written.

Microsoft Word 2010 includes a number of picture tools that help you fine-tune your pictures and add professional, artistic touches that can really make your work stand out. New features in Word 2010 enable you to add artistic effects—including all kinds of special filters—to the images you add. And the enhanced cropping tool makes it simple for you to display just the aspect of your image that is sure to get the most attention.

A Quick Look at Word 2010 Illustrations

Years ago, adding a photo or a diagram to a document was a pretty big deal. Today it's very easy to do and what's more, you can apply all sorts of professional effects to make the images look great on the page. In the Illustrations group of the Insert tab, Word 2010 gives you the tools to add several different types of illustrations to your document so that you can inspire your readers with photographs, drawings, charts, diagrams, screenshots, and more.

Pictures

Chances are that you'll use the Picture tool quite a bit. Using this tool, you can add photos or other artwork you've already saved in folders on your computer. Once you put the picture in place, you can use Word's picture editing tools to fine-tune its appearance.

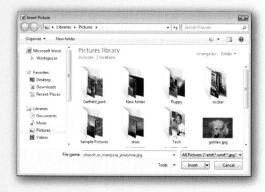

Clip Art

Word 2010 offers a large collection of clip art—with more being posted all the time—and connects directly to Office.com so you can always access the great number of downloadable art available for free online. And clip art isn't just cartoons—you'll also find photos and sound and video clips available through the Clip Art tool.

Shapes

If you want to create your own illustrations in your document, Word 2010 offers a large collection of ready-made shapes you can add directly to your page. You can create a drawing canvas and add the custom illustration there or simply click the shape you want and draw right on the page.

Charts

You can create and insert a variety of chart types directly into your Word documents using the Chart tool in the Illustrations group. A datasheet enables you to add and modify chart values; you can customize the chart to add titles, labels, values, formatting, and more.

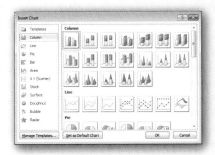

SmartArt

SmartArt graphics give you a simple way to create professional-looking diagrams, helping you illustrate key ideas in the documents you create. SmartArt offers a number of different diagram styles, and you can customize all the diagrams you create within each style type.

Screenshots

A new feature in Word 2010 enables you to capture and insert screenshots in your Word documents. You might do this, for example, when you want to show a picture of your business Web site or when you are illustrating a book like this one.

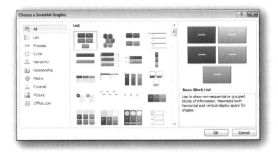

Inserting a Picture

Adding pictures to your document livens things up and gives your readers something colorful to capture their interest. If you're creating a dry report, you can include a photo of key staff members to personalize the document. If you're writing Web copy, you can add images of your building, the surrounding landscape, your products, or happy customers to paint a positive image of what you do. Inserting a picture is a simple task in Word, and Word accepts images in a number of different file formats, as you can see in the following table. This means you can use pictures from a wide variety of sources—nothing goes to waste!

Picture Format Name	File Format
Windows Enhanced Metafile	.emf
Windows Metafile	.wmf
JPEG File Interchange Format	.jpg, .jpeg, .jfif, .jpe
Portable Network Graphics	.png
Windows Bitmap	.bmp, .dib, .rle
Graphics Interchange Format	.gif, .gfa
Compressed Windows Enhanced Metafile	.emz
Compressed Windows Metafile	.wmz
Compressed Macintosh PICT	.pcz
Tag Image File Format	.tif, .tiff
WordPerfect Graphics	.wpg
Computer Graphics Metafile	.cgm
Encapsulated PostScript	.eps
Macintosh PICT	.pct, .pict

See Also

"Adding Clip Art" on page 134 for information about inserting pictures that you've cataloged using the Clip Organizer.

Try This!

Most of us today have lots of digital pictures, and Office 2010 comes with a valuable tool that can help you manage your media effectively. The Microsoft Office Picture Manager is available in Microsoft Office Tools. Simply click Start, click All Programs, click Microsoft Office, and choose Microsoft Office Tools. Click Microsoft Office Picture Manager to open the software and begin working with your photos.

Insert a Picture

(1) Click in your document where you want to insert the picture.

(2) On the Insert tab, click the Picture button in the Illustrations group to display the Insert Picture window.

(3) Navigate to the folder that contains the picture you want and click the picture file.

(4) Click the down arrow next to the Insert button and click one of the following:

- Insert to copy the picture and store it in the Word document.

- Link To File to connect to the picture file without increasing the file size of your Word document. (The source picture file must be available for the picture to be displayed.)

- Insert And Link to copy the picture, store it in the Word document, and update the picture automatically whenever the source picture file changes.

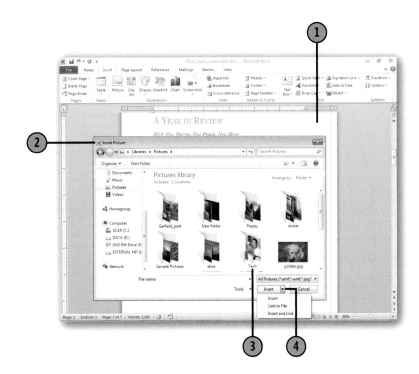

See Also

"Editing and Formatting a Picture" on page 137 for information about modifying a picture or its placement.

Changing the Size of a Picture

Pictures come in all shapes and sizes, and depending on how you have your digital camera options set (or where you found your images), your pictures might be extremely large. When you insert them on your page, they may overwhelm your text.

There are two different ways you can get your pictures down to a manageable size—you can resize the entire image or you can crop the image to just the part you want. Or, of course, both.

Crop It

① Click the picture and click the Picture Tools Format tab.

② Click Crop in the Size group.

③ Place the cropping mouse cursor over a cropping handle and drag the sides, top, or bottom of the picture to crop off the parts you don't want.

④ Click outside the image to turn off cropping.

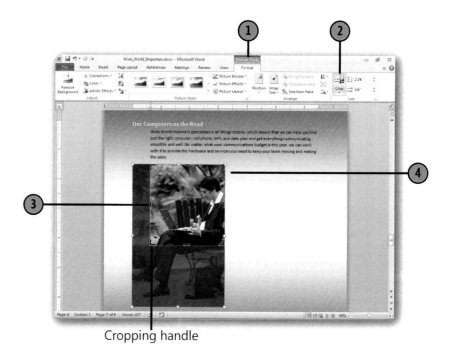

Cropping handle

Size It

① Click to select the picture if it isn't already selected.

② Drag a Sizing handle on the picture to modify the size of the picture.

③ Click outside the image to complete the process.

Sizing handle

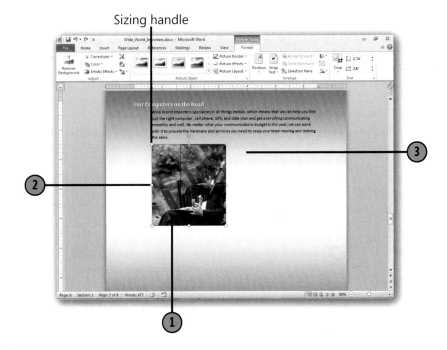

Try This!

Now in Word 2010 you can crop a photo to a shape to add special touches to your files. Add a photo to your page by clicking Insert, Picture, and choosing the photo you want to add. Click Insert to paste the photo at the cursor position. Now click the photo and click the Picture Tools Format tab. In the Size group, click the Crop arrow, and point to Crop To Shape. Click the shape you want to apply to the photo and watch what happens on your page! The photo is cropped to the shape you selected. You won't want to use this often in your publications and worksheets, but once in a while it's a fun feature.

Tip

If you want to crop your photo to a specific shape, you can set the aspect ratio before you crop. To do this, click the Picture Tools Format tab and click the Crop arrow in the Size group. Point to Aspect Ratio and click the ratio you want to apply to the image.

Adding Clip Art

Word 2010 gives you access to clip art, photographs, video, and audio clips that are included with the program as well as a whole world full of clips available online at Office.com. When you search for a specific illustration you'd like to use for your document, you can enter a simple word or phrase—*computer*, for example—and the Clip Art tool will provide you with dozens of results to review. When you add a picture to a document, the picture becomes part of the document, and you can edit and change it as you'd like.

Find and Insert Clip Art

1. Click in your document where you want to place the clip art.

2. On the Insert tab, click Clip Art in the Illustrations group.

3. In the Clip Art pane, type a keyword or keywords to describe the type of picture you want.

4. Specify the type of clip you want.

5. Click to include clips from Office.com in the search.

6. Click Go to view the items that match your criteria.

7. Click to insert the picture into your document. Add any other clip art you want, and close the Clip Art pane when you've finished.

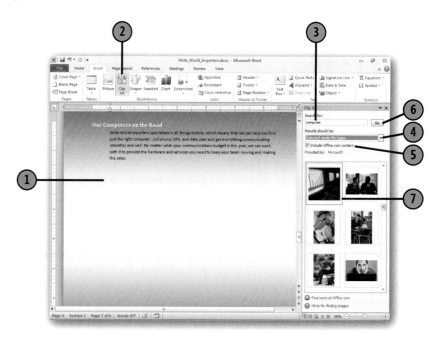

See Also

"Changing the Size of a Picture" on page 132 for information about cropping and resizing the clip art.

See Also

"Editing and Formatting a Picture" on page 137 for information about modifying the clip art.

Adding Shapes

For some documents you may want to draw things yourself. Word 2010 includes a palette of shapes you can use to create all sorts of images—buttons, boxes, and much more—on your page. You can use shapes as containers for text and create pull quotes, sidebars, coupons—almost anything you can envision you can create. Once you've drawn the shape, you can add 3-D effects, shadows, or special formatting touches to make the shape stand out.

Draw a Shape

① Click in your document where you want to insert the shape.

② On the Insert tab, click Shapes in the Illustrations group, and choose the shape you want from the gallery that appears.

③ Hold down the left mouse button, and drag out the shape.

(continued on next page)

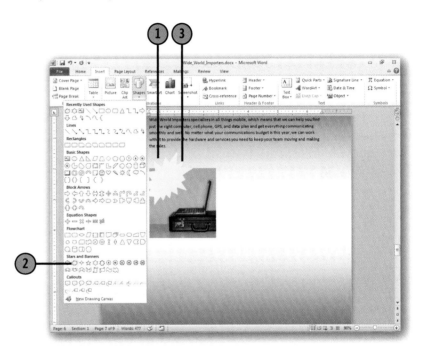

Draw a Shape *(continued)*

④ Adjust the shape by dragging the

- Sizing handles to change the size of the drawing.

- Adjustment handle to reshape the drawing.

- Rotation handle to rotate the drawing.

⑤ Change the shape fill and outline color.

⑥ Use Shape Effects to apply special effects—including shadow, glow, and more—to the shape.

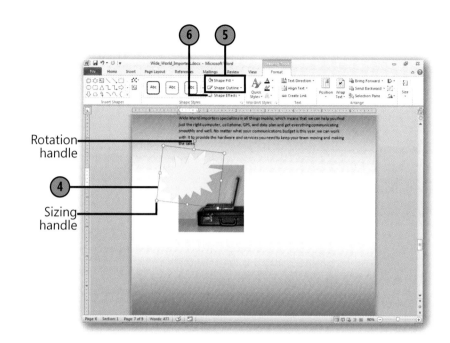

Rotation handle

Sizing handle

See Also

"Adding Shapes" on page 135 for information about modifying the appearance of a shape.

See Also

"Arranging Multiple Graphics" on page 144 for information about combining multiple shapes for special effects.

See Also

"Creating Artistic Text" on page 148 and "Adding Text Boxes" on pages 87–89 for information about customizing the text and text layout in a text box.

Editing and Formatting a Picture

Word 2010 includes some great picture editing tools that enable you to fine-tune your images, adjusting brightness, contrast, and color. In addition to picture editing tools, you can apply special artistic effects to give your pictures a professional appearance, displaying them, for example, as watercolor prints, ink drawings, or even images through glass. Using these types of special picture enhancements help you create a document your readers will remember.

Change Its Appearance

1 Click the picture and click the Picture Tools Format tab.

2 Click Corrections.

3 Click the setting you want to apply to the image.

Tip

When you edit a picture, you're editing only the copy of it that you've inserted into your Word document. If you want to change the original picture file, you'll need to edit it in a separate program—for example, in Windows Paint or Microsoft Office Picture Manager.

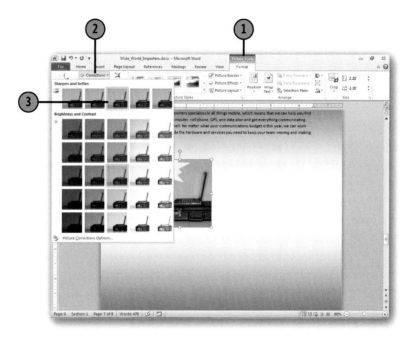

Format a Picture

1. Click the picture you want to format.

2. Click the Picture Tools Format tab.

3. Click the More button in the lower-right corner of the Picture Styles gallery to display all your choices, and click the style you want to apply.

4. Click Picture Border to choose a new color for the border or change border style.

5. Click Picture Effects to add or change the 3-D rotation, shadow, reflection, glow, or soft edges.

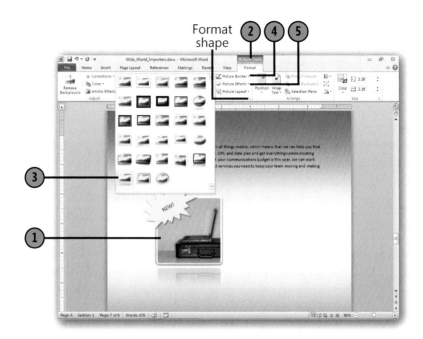

Tip

If you want to set precise values for brightness, contrast, shadows, or 3-D settings, including rotation, click the Format Shape button. To rotate a picture 90 or 180 degrees, click the Rotate button in the Arrange section of the ribbon.

Getting Artistic with Pictures

You've probably noticed that documents get better looking all the time. Changes in technology have made it possible for us to take lots of pictures and include those pictures in the work we produce. Word 2010 includes a great new feature called Artistic Effects that makes it simple for you to create unique and professional effects for your pictures. You can apply all

sorts of different filters to create different looks and give new life—and lots of visual appeal—to the pictures you include on your pages. You can also recolor the pictures you use to create special picture effects that correspond to other colors used in your document.

Apply Artistic Effects

(1) Click the picture in your document.

(2) Click the Picture Tools Format tab.

(3) Click Artistic Effects and hover the mouse over the different effects.

(4) Click the effect you want to apply.

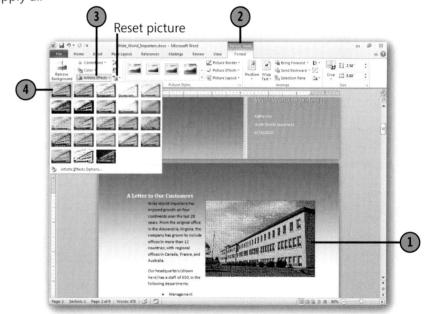

Reset picture

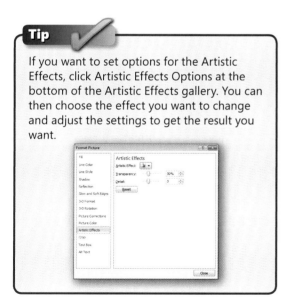

Caution

The Reset Picture button resets all the changes you've made, including any cropping or sizing. If you want to undo only one or two changes, use the Undo button on the Quick Access toolbar.

Tip

If you don't like the result of the effect you've applied, click Reset Picture to reset the entire picture to the way it looked when you first inserted it.

Recolor a Picture

① Click the picture you want to change.

② Click the Picture Tools Format tab.

③ Click Color in the Adjust group.

④ Click the type of recoloring adjustment you want to apply.

Tip

You can adjust settings individually by clicking Picture Color Options at the bottom of the Color gallery.

Color Saturation controls the amount of color used.

Color Tone sets the temperature of the color.

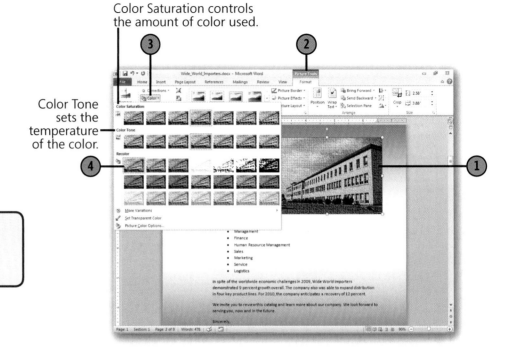

Removing Picture Backgrounds

Many of the pictures we create include elements we'd like to leave out. A great picture of your dog, for example, might include the foot of a friend, the mess in the corner, or a product you'd rather not showcase in your document. Word 2010 includes a great new feature than enables you to remove the background of the picture so your readers' attention is drawn just to the part you want them to see.

Remove Picture Background

① Click the picture you want to change.

② Click the Picture Tools Format tab.

③ In the Adjust group, click Remove Background.

④ Click Mark Areas To Keep, Mark Areas To Remove, or Delete Mark as needed to adjust the purple masking (this is the background area that will be removed).

⑤ When the picture is marked the way you want it, click Keep Changes.

⑥ To reset the picture and return the background, click Discard All Changes.

Tip ✓

Using the Remove Background command takes a little practice, but it enables you to create some professional effects and fun pictures for the documents and publications you create.

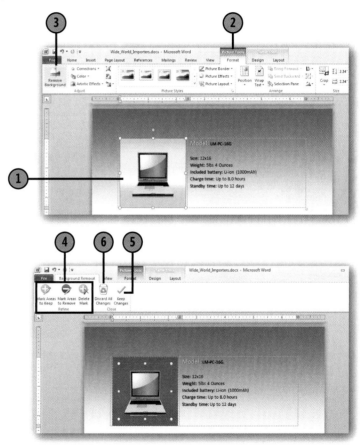

Wrapping Text Around a Graphic

When you place images, shapes, pictures, and diagrams in your document, you need to be able to adjust the text to make room for those items. Wrapping text around an item adds another level of polish to your document. However, using one of the standard text-wrapping configurations doesn't always produce the desired effect. As you might expect, you can customize the way Word wraps the text.

Set the Text Wrapping

(1) Click the picture.

(2) Click the Picture Tools Format tab and click the Wrap Text in the Arrange group. Click the text-wrapping option you want.

(3) Drag the picture to set its position in the paragraph. The text wraps around it.

(4) If the text wrapping still doesn't look the way you want, click the Text Wrapping button again, choose More Layout Options from the menu, and make your custom layout settings in the Advanced Layout dialog box. Click OK when you've finished.

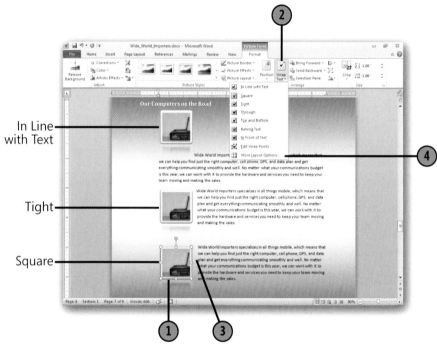

In Line with Text

Tight

Square

Tip

When you're using the drawing canvas, set the text wrapping for the drawing canvas itself, not for the individual items on the canvas.

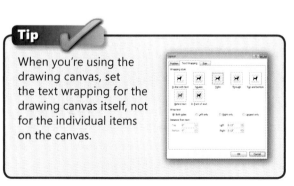

Change the Wrapping Shape

1. Click to select the item to be wrapped if it isn't already selected.

2. Click the Text Wrapping button, and choose either Tight or Through text wrapping. Click the Text Wrapping button again, and choose Edit Wrap Points from the menu.

3. Drag a wrapping point to change the wrapping outline. Continue moving wrapping points, or drag the line to create a new wrapping point.

4. Click outside the item to deselect it.

Wrap Part of an Item

1. Click at the point where you want to stop the wrap.

2. On the Page Layout tab, click the Breaks button, and click the Text Wrapping option.

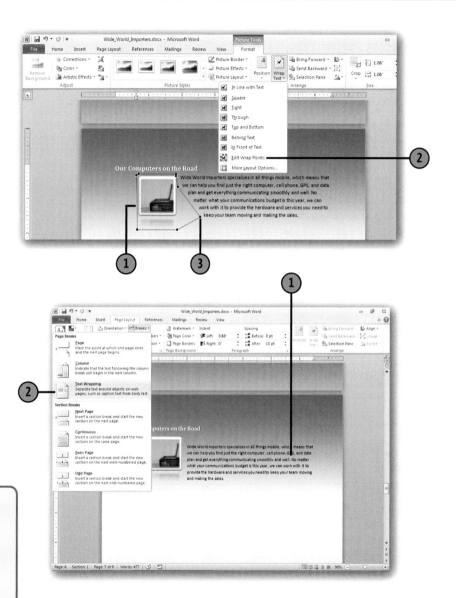

Try This!

Set an item with Behind Text wrapping, move the item so that the text runs over it, and try to select the item. No luck? Click the Select button on the Home tab, choose Select Objects from the menu, and drag a selection rectangle around the item. Now you can move the item or change its wrap. Click the Select button again and click Select Objects to turn it off.

Arranging Multiple Graphics

When you have more than one graphic (or type of graphic) in your document—for example, pictures, clip art, and/or shapes that are meant to appear together—you can arrange them in whatever configuration you want. You may want to overlap the graphics so that one appears in front of another or group several items into one group so that you can move, resize, and copy and paste them together.

Arrange the Graphics

① Click a graphic and click the Picture Tools Format tab.

② Click Bring Forward or Send Backward in the Arrange group to arrange the image.

③ Repeat for other graphics on the page.

(continued on next page)

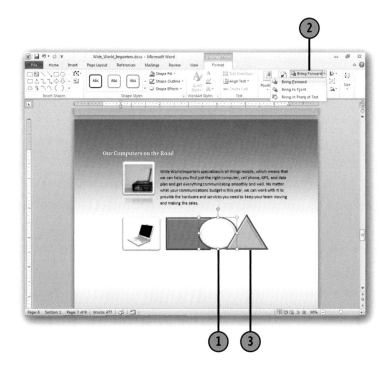

Arrange the Graphics *(continued)*

④ Select multiple shapes by pressing Ctrl and clicking each item.

⑤ Click Group in the Arrange group to combine the shapes into a single object.

> **Tip**
>
> You can ungroup items you've put together by clicking the group, clicking the Picture Tools Format or Drawing Tools Format contextual tab, clicking the Group tool, and choosing Ungroup.

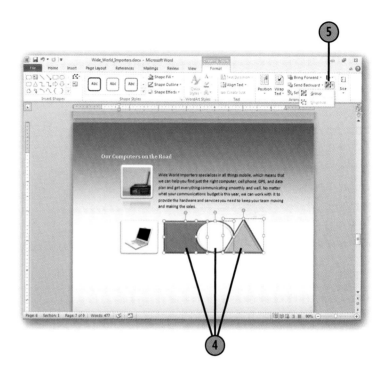

Positioning Graphics on the Page

Your readers expect to see some kind of logical order on your page, so no matter how great your images look, you can't just put them haphazardly on the page. You can use Word 2010's alignment tools to make sure your images appear just where you want them to in the document.

Align to the Page

1. Select the image. Click the Picture Tools Format tab or the Drawing Tools Format tab.

2. Click Align in the Arrange group and choose View Gridlines.

3. Click the Align button again, and specify whether you want the graphic to align relative to the edge of the paper or to the margin.

4. Click the Align button again, and click where you want to place the graphic on the page.

5. To fine-tune its position, drag the graphic to where you want it, using the grid to align the graphic to other items.

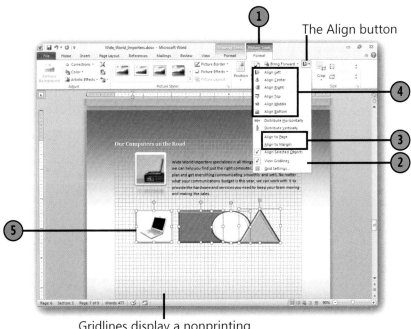

The Align button

Gridlines display a nonprinting layout grid on the page.

Align Pictures with Each Other

(1) Click the pictures you want to align by holding down the Ctrl key as you click each one.

(2) Click Align.

(3) Align Selected Objects.

(4) Click the item that reflects the way you want the pictures to align.

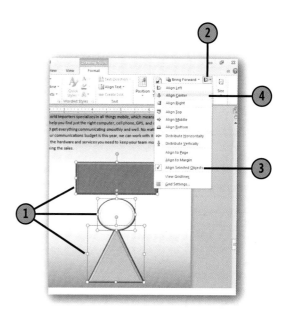

Creating Artistic Text

Word 2010 includes features that help you stylize your text in new ways. WordArt is a tool that has been around for a while, but it is more closely integrated into the workings of Word now. You can add all kinds of effects, curving your text words and phrases, creating interesting angles, shadows, and more.

Add WordArt Elements

① On the Insert tab, click WordArt in the Text group to display the Word-Art gallery.

② Click the WordArt style you want.

③ A text box appears on your page with the format you selected. Click in the box.

④ Type your text.

⑤ Click outside the text box.

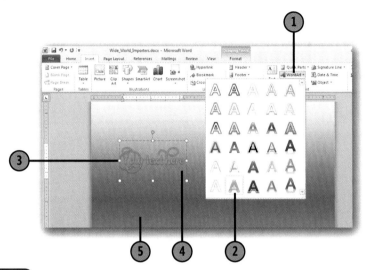

Tip

You can turn regular text into WordArt by selecting the text before you click the WordArt tool.

Try This!

Create some WordArt, select it, and then use the tools on the WordArt Tools Format tab to change the shape, character spacing and height, and text alignment. Use the WordArt Styles gallery to apply a three-dimensional effect. Use the 3-D Effects tools to change the color, depth, direction, lighting, surface type, and 3-D angle. Amazing, isn't it? And so much fun!

Tip

You may notice that the styles available in the Text Effects gallery (in the Font group of the Home tab) and the styles available in WordArt look similar. You're right—they do. But WordArt creates a text box with the phrase "Your text here," and in order to edit and format the object you use the Drawing Tools Format contextual tab. Text effects add and format the text on your document page, so the result is that the actual text is given the format you choose from Text Effects.

Inserting a Relational Diagram

SmartArt is the diagramming tool in Word 2010 that makes it easy for you to show relationships—including comparisons, processes, and more—in your documents. SmartArt offers a number of different categories with different styles of diagrams you can adapt to fit what you want to show. You can also use pictures as part of the diagram (this is a new feature in Word 2010) and continue to add to the diagram as your needs change.

Create a Diagram

1. Click the Insert tab and click SmartArt in the Illustrations group.

2. Select the type of diagram you want.

3. Click a diagram design, review the information about that diagram, and click OK to create the diagram.

(continued on next page)

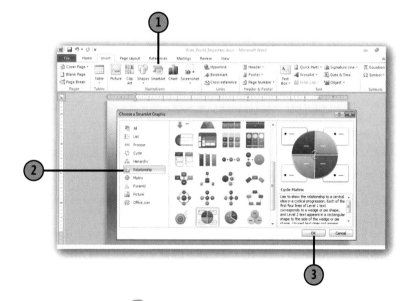

Tip

You can't create SmartArt graphics in a Word 97–2003 format document. When you save a document that contains SmartArt in the Word 97–2003 format, the SmartArt is converted into a picture that you can't modify.

④ Click Change Colors in the Smart Styles group of the SmartArt Tools Design tab and select the color palette you want to use.

⑤ Click the first item in the Text pane and type the text for that item. If the Text pane isn't displayed, click Text Pane on the SmartArt Tools Design tab.

⑥ Continue entering text, doing any of the following:

- Press the Tab key to make the entry a subentry of the previous item (or click Demote), or Press Shift+Tab to elevate the entry one level (or click Promote).

- Press Enter to finish the current item and insert a new line for text.

- Press the Down arrow key to move to the next item.

- Press Delete to remove entries you don't want.

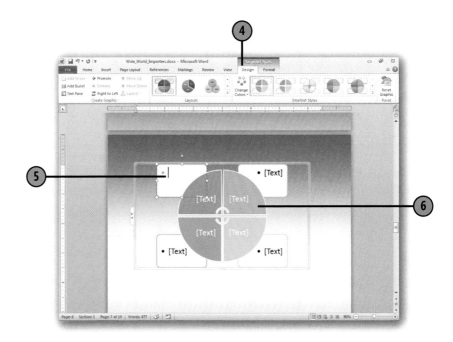

Modify the Diagram

1. On the SmartArt Tools Design tab, point to different layouts and click the one that works best for your content.

2. Point to different SmartArt Styles and click the one you want.

3. Use the SmartArt Tools Format tab to set text and shape formats.

4. Click the frame of the diagram and use a Sizing handle to change the diagram's size.

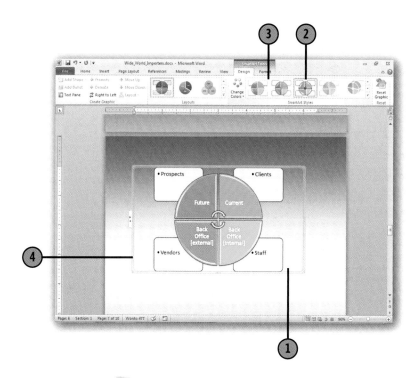

Try This!

Create a list in your document. Select the text and copy it (press Ctrl+C). Insert a SmartArt diagram. Click in the Text pane and press Ctrl+V to paste your copied text. Edit the text, setting any levels you want. Point to different layouts to see which layout works best with your content.

Creating a Chart

One of the beautiful things about the various programs in Office 2010 is that it is so easy to use the programs together. When you're working with data that you'd like to present in a chart, you can easily add a chart within Word that draws from the powerful features of Excel. The process is simple, and the chart will look great with just a few clicks of the mouse.

Create a Chart

1. Click the Insert tab and click Chart in the Illustrations group.

2. Select a chart type.

3. Click the chart design you want and click OK.

(continued on next page)

Tip

If you don't have Excel installed on your computer, Microsoft Graph will start when you click the Chart button on the Insert tab. Microsoft Graph works much like Excel, although it has fewer features.

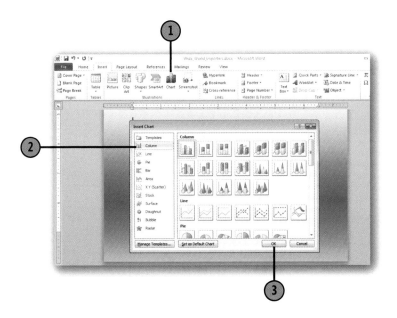

Create a Chart *(continued)*

4 In the Excel worksheet that appears, edit the sample data so that only your data is shown.

5 The result of your data entry appears in the chart.

6 Close the worksheet when you've finished.

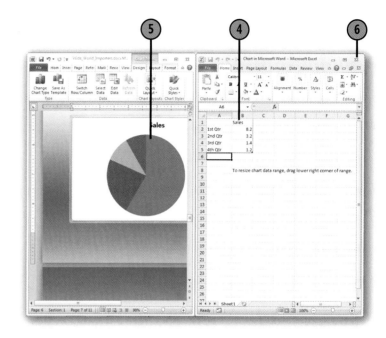

Format the Chart

(1) Click in the chart to select it if it isn't already selected.

(2) If you need to modify which data is shown and how it's organized, on the Chart Tools Design tab, click the Edit Data button, and make your modifications in the worksheet that appears.

(3) Use the tools on the Chart Tools Design tab to change the chart type, the data, the layout, and the overall appearance of the chart.

(4) Use the tools on the Chart Tools Layout tab to add annotations, labels, and other elements.

(5) Use the tools on the Chart Tools Format tab to format individual items in the chart.

(6) Save the document to save the data and the design of the chart.

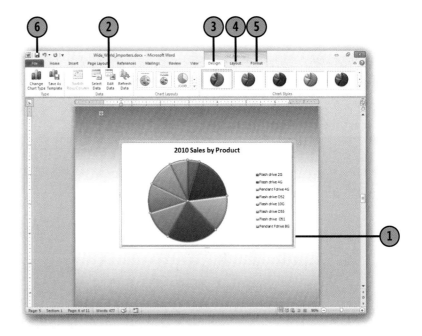

Although the Excel worksheet looks like a standard worksheet, it's actually a special Excel object that's stored in your Word file. All your chart information and data are stored in the Word file, so you don't need to access the Excel file to view or modify the chart in Word.

Word 2010 for Blogging, Mailing, and More

Whether you've been working with computers for a long time or you're relatively new to the game, you are no doubt aware that today we're using Word to create much more than documents you print on the printer and share with co-workers and friends. Whether you want to create a blog post, prepare a Web page, complete a mass mailing, print envelopes, or send notes to your OneNote notebook, Microsoft Word 2010 includes the features to help you produce the end result you're imagining.

This section is all about using Word to complete tasks outside those more traditional write-edit-print documents you may create. Along the way, you'll find out about the variety of file formats you will work with as you create your Word projects and learn the ins and outs of creating a form letter and customizing it so the recipient feels you're writing to him or her personally (which, of course, you are).

Composing Different Types of Documents

Word 2010 includes dozens of templates that offer all kinds of different documents you can create. Click the New tab in Backstage view and you'll see a large collection of document categories from which you can choose. Reports? Sure. Invitations? You bet. Whether you want newsletters or agendas or any kind of document you'll share in paper or electronically, you can find it in Word's templates.

Search for a template type.

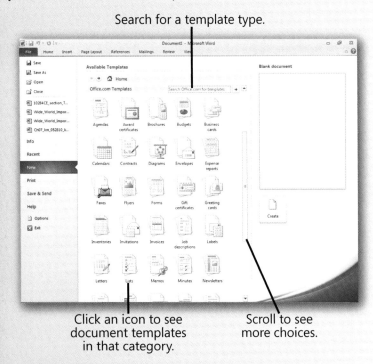

Click an icon to see document templates in that category.

Scroll to see more choices.

See Also

"Designing a Template" on page 100 for information about creating your own templates.

What are the main differences you should be concerned with when you plan to create a document that you'll share electronically instead of in print? The biggest difference is that you don't need to worry about some of the traditional page setup issues:

- Page margins
- Columns
- Headers and footers
- Page numbers
- Orientation

See Also

"Create a Template from Scratch" on page 101 for more information about selecting the template you want to use to create your document.

Tip

If you want to create a document that will be viewed electronically but also may be printed, you do want to set up the page as though it will be sent to the printer. This means you can include page margins, columns, headers and footers, page numbers, and more. Then the reader can view the document on the screen but also print it if desired. For some documents, it's nice to have the choice.

Other issues you *do* need to think about as you plan a nontraditional document are these:

- How are your readers likely to view the file?

- Do you want readers to be able to edit or modify the electronic version?

- Will you include hyperlinks so readers can move from page to page and document to document?

- In what format should you save it?

See Also

"Customizing a Template" on page 98 for information about modifying a template.

Caution

A paragraph mark contains the paragraph's formatting, so don't delete a paragraph mark unless you want to remove that paragraph's elements from your document. When you delete a paragraph mark, any special formatting that was designed for that paragraph will be lost.

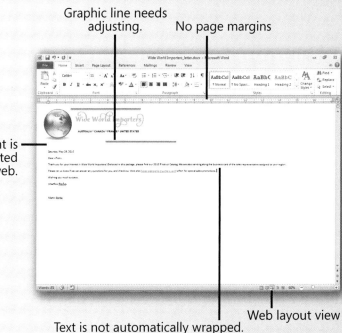

Page margins and indents in effect

Graphic line needs adjusting.

No page margins

Document is formatted for the web.

Portrait orientation

Text margin

Print layout view

Web layout view

Text is not automatically wrapped.

Word's File Formats

When you plan to share files with others, thinking through the format you use to save the file is very important. Word 2010 uses some different file formats from those of versions of Word prior to Word 2007, but with a few simple steps you can make sure that's not a problem for others who work in different file formats. If you decide not to use the new formats, however, be aware that you won't be able to use some of Word's very cool new features. Review the descriptions of the formats to see which work best for you. To see the list of available formats, choose Save As from the File menu, and, in the Save As dialog box, scroll through the Save As Type list.

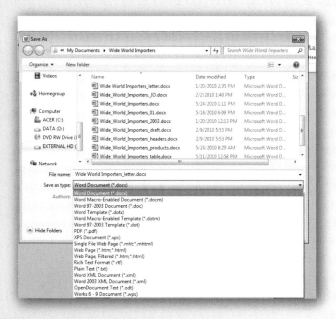

Word's New File Formats

- **Word Document:** This is the new format that enables all of Word's new features. Documents in this format can't be opened in earlier versions of Word unless you've downloaded and installed a special translating filter program. The Word Document format has the file extension .docx and saves files in the eXtensible Markup Language (XML) format. A single Word document has multiple XML files, but Word places them in a single container.

- **Word Macro-Enabled Document:** This is the same format as the Word Document format, except that it contains macros. This special file type is a security enhancement, and it allows system managers and others to restrict the use of macros that could carry viruses and other evil things.

- **Word XML Document:** This is a plain text file that includes all the text and the XML coding. This format is used primarily in a corporate setting in which transforms are created to extract and/or reformat information that will be stored for reuse.

- **Word Template:** This new form of template also enables the new features of Word and, as in the Word Document format, stores multiple XML files in a single containing file with the .dotx file extension.

- **Word Macro-Enabled Template:** This is the same format as the Word Template format, except that it can contain macros.

Word's Other File Formats

- **Word 97–2003 Document:** This is the binary file format used in previous versions of Word. It provides compatibility with earlier versions of Word, but saving in this format disables some of the advanced features of Word 2007.

- **Word 97–2003 Template:** This is the binary file format used in previous versions of Word. Macros, AutoText, custom toolbars, and styles are stored in this file.

- **Single File Web Page:** This format creates a Web page and stores all the graphics in the same file.

- **Web Page:** This format creates a standard HTML–format Web page whose graphics are stored in a separate folder.

- **Web Page, Filtered:** This format creates a standard HTML–format Web page, which deletes Word-specific information that isn't needed to display the Web page. Any graphics in the document are stored in a separate folder.

- **Rich Text Format:** This is a binary file that contains the text and formatting information but little else. It provides compatibility with many programs, including WordPad and earlier versions of Word.

- **Plain Text:** This text file contains only the text of the document and no formatting.

- **Word 2003 XML Document:** This format saves a document in the XML format compatible with Word 2003 XML schemas.

- **Works 6.0–9.0:** This format provides compatibility with people who use the Microsoft Works word processor.

See Also

Ensure that colleagues and friends can read your documents. See the section "Work in Compatibility Mode" on page 40 to make sure others can view what's most important in your Word 2010 document.

Creating an Online Document

Creating a document that will be posted for others to read online is a snap in Word 2010. An effective online Word document includes hyperlinks that enable readers to easily navigate to other parts of the current document or to other documents or Web pages. The document may also include e-mail links and also include other documents or files as icons in the current file so that readers can quickly move to relevant information that is related to the document you've posted. When you're finished with the file, you can easily save it as a Web page, give it a title, and post it to your server space.

Add an E-mail Address

① Highlight the text in the document where you want to add the e-mail link.

② Click the Insert tab and click Hyperlink in the Links group (or press Ctrl+K).

③ Click E-mail Address.

④ Type the e-mail address.

⑤ Type the text you want to include in the subject line of the e-mail message.

⑥ Click to add a ScreenTip providing prompt text when the user hovers the mouse over the address.

⑦ Click OK.

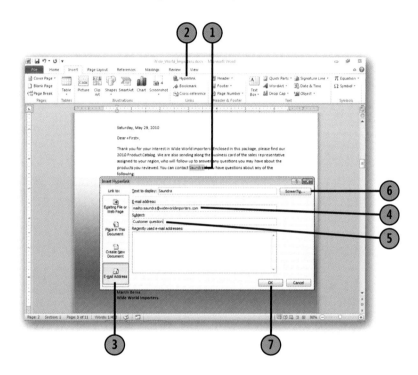

Save as a Web Page

1. Finish the document as usual.
2. Click the File tab and click Save As.
3. Click the Save As Type arrow and choose Web Page.
4. Click Change Title.
5. Type a title for the page and click OK.
6. Click to add tags that help identify your page in a search.
7. Click and type a name for the page and click Save.

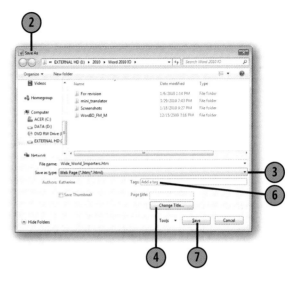

Including a File Within a File

In some cases, you may want to share additional resource files within the online document you are preparing for colleagues or team members. You might, for example, insert the letter you want to send to new customers and ask your peers to review it along with the newest sales brochure. You can easily include a file as a simple icon so readers can click the icon to display the file if they choose. If they'd rather not view the file, it doesn't take up much room in the document or interrupt the flow of your text.

Add a Text Object

① Click in the document where you want to add the file.

② To insert an entire file as an icon, click the Object tool in the Text group of the Insert tab.

③ Click the Create From File tab, click Browse, locate the file, and click Insert.

④ Select this check box.

⑤ If you want to use a different icon, click Change Icon, select a different icon or type a new caption, and click OK.

⑥ Click OK in the Object dialog box.

(continued on next page)

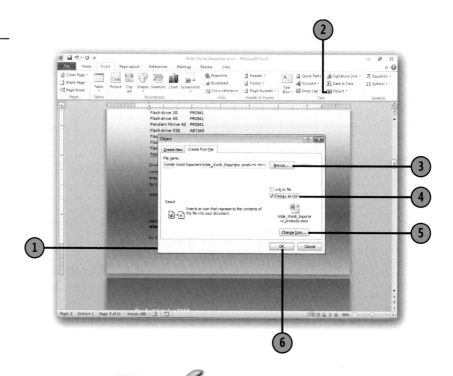

See Also

"Adding Hyperlinks" on page 23 to learn how to add hyperlinks in your document.

Tip

You can include any type of file as an icon: a video, a sound clip, an Excel file, a PowerPoint presentation, and so on. Readers of your online document must have the proper programs installed to be able to open these files.

Add a Text Object *(continued)*

⑦ Move the file icon to the place you want it to appear. Set the text wrapping for the icon, if desired. Set any document protection you want, and then save and distribute the document.

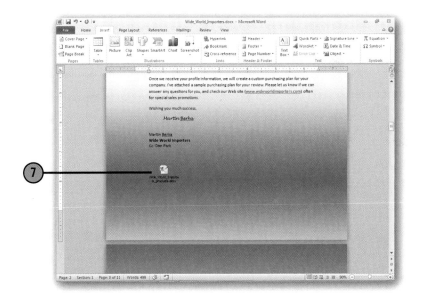

Caution

If your online document includes hyperlinks to other documents, make sure that the recipients of your document have access to the linked files. If you're uncertain about this, include the original documents and display them as icons.

Writing and Publishing a Blog

Well, who doesn't know about the blogosphere? Blogs are a popular way for individuals and companies to share information—free and continuously—with the Web-browsing public. Not everyone wants or needs a blog, of course, but a blog does provide a simple—and sometimes fun—way to share bits of information about a topic you care about. A Web log, *blog*, is a Web-based site where you can add your entries, called posts, which you can create in Word. The great thing about creating blog entries in Word is that you can use all Word's tools for checking the spelling and grammar, translating words and phrases, and formatting as you'd like; then you can publish the post directly to your blog.

Set Up Your Blog

1 Click the File tab and click New.

2 Click Blog Post.

3 Choose Create.

(continued on next page)

Tip

Confused by the terminology? The word *blog* as a noun refers to the online site where you post your writing. The word *blog* is also used as a verb, as in "I'm going to *blog* about the new Translation features."

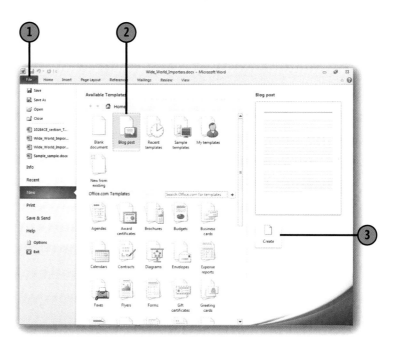

Set Up Your Blog *(continued)*

④ If this is the first time you're using Word to post to your blog, click Register Now in the Register A Blog Account dialog box. In the New Blog Account Wizard that appears, select the service you're using and click Next.

⑤ Choose the blogging service you use and click Next.

⑥ Complete your account information. The details you're asked to provide will vary depending on the service you're using, but will likely require your user name and password, the URL (Web address) of your blog, and possibly the type of blog interface you're using.

⑦ Click the Picture Options button to display the Picture Options dialog box and choose how you want pictures to be added.

⑧ Click OK in each of the dialog boxes.

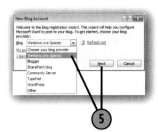

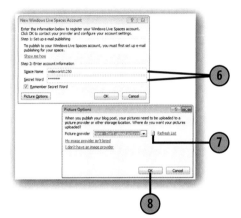

Tip

Many, but not all, public blog hosts support direct publishing. If your blog isn't supported by one of these hosts, write your content in Word, copy it, and then paste it into the blog's editing window.

Create a Blog Entry

① On the Blog Post tab, click the Post Title content control and type the title for this blog entry. Use any of the formatting tools to format the title the way you want it.

② If you want to include a category for the entry, click the Insert Category button, enter the name and password for your account, if necessary, and then choose a category from the drop-down list that appears.

③ Click in the body of the document and enter your text, using styles or direct formatting.

④ Use the items on the Insert tab to insert special content, including tables, pictures, shapes, and hyperlinks.

⑤ Click Publish to publish the entry on your blog. If you want to send the entry to your blog as a draft so that you can view it there before you publish it, click the down arrow at the bottom of the Publish button, and choose Publish As Draft from the drop-down menu.

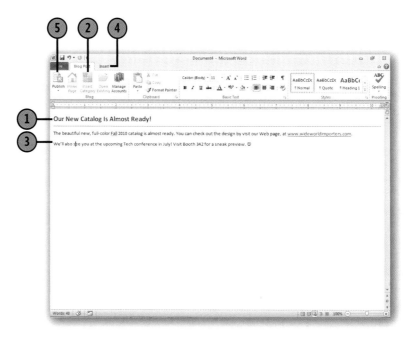

Tip

Click the Manage Accounts button to select a different blog account or to change the settings for your account. Click the Open Existing button to review your past blog postings.

Tip

Click the Home Page button to go to your blog site, and verify that the blog appears as you want it. If you published the entry as a draft, sign in if necessary and use the tools on your blog site to edit and publish the draft.

Printing an Envelope

In some cases, adding a handwritten envelope may be just the touch you're looking for, but in other cases—especially when you're sending business correspondence—a printed envelope makes your document look more professional.

Word makes it easy for you to create crisp, businesslike printed envelopes. You can easily include your return address, and in the United States you can add electronic postage so you can avoid stamps altogether. If you already have the delivery address in your letter, Word usually detects it and copies it to the Envelopes And Labels dialog box. You can also type the address directly in the dialog box.

Add the Address

① Click the Mailings tab and click Envelopes in the Create group to display the Envelopes and Labels dialog box.

② If a delivery address is displayed on the Envelopes tab, verify that it's correct.

③ If no delivery address is shown or if you want to use a different address, type the address. If the address is in your Microsoft Outlook Contacts list, click the Insert Address button.

④ Verify that the return address is correct. If you're using an envelope with a preprinted return address, select the Omit check box so that the return address won't be printed.

⑤ Click Options.

⑥ On the Envelope Options tab, specify the envelope size and the fonts and positions for the addresses.

⑦ On the Printing Options tab, specify how the envelope is to be loaded and printed. Click OK.

⑧ If you have Electronic Postage (E-Postage) software installed, select this check box to use electronic postage.

⑨ If you need to make changes to your E-Postage setup, click the E-Postage Properties button.

⑩ Click Print to print the envelope.

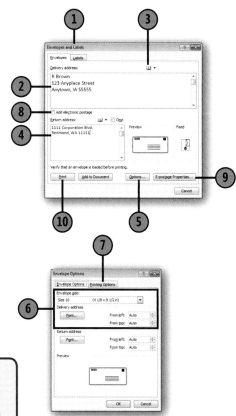

Tip

Your return address is based on the user information Word has stored for you. You can change it in the Envelopes And Labels dialog box, and Word will then change it in the user information.

Printing a Mailing Label

Printing mailing labels can be a real time-saver when you need to send many copies of a document—letter, newsletter, brochure, or report—to people at different addresses. In the past, mailing labels could be a bit of a headache, but Word 2010 makes the whole process simple for you. All you need to do is specify the type of label you're using, the address, and the way you want the label to be printed. That's it! Word does the rest. You can also use this method to print other types of labels, from business card labels to CD labels.

Print a Label

1. Note the manufacturer and the number of the labels you have (for example, Avery 5332). If you're planning to print only one label, figure out which label on the sheet of labels is the one you're going to use. Later in the process, you'll need to specify the label by row (the horizontal line of labels) and by column (the vertical line of labels). Insert the sheet of labels into your printer (usually into the manual feed tray if your printer has one).

2. Click the Mailings tab and click Labels to display the Envelopes And Labels dialog box.

3. Click the Labels tab and use the proposed address, type a new one, or click the Insert Address button to insert an address from your Outlook Contacts list. To insert your return address, select the Use Return Address check box.

4. If the type of label shown isn't the one you're using, click here to display the Label Options dialog box, specify the label you're using and click OK.

5. Click the appropriate option to print a whole page of identical labels or only one label on the sheet of labels. If you want to print only one label, specify the label by row and column.

6. Click Print to print your label or labels.

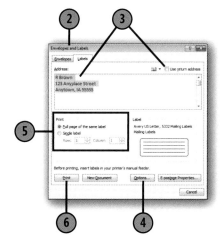

Tip

If you need to print a large number of different mailing labels, consider using the mail merge feature.

See Also

"Mail Merge: The Power and the Pain" on page 169, and "Creating a Form Letter" on page 170, for the ins and outs of running a successful mail merge.

Mail Merge: The Power and the Pain

If you've ever had to send the same letter or catalog to more than one person, you know what a time-saver mail merge can be. Mail merge saves you the trouble of typing numerous names and addresses by merging your contacts list with the document you're creating. In Word 2010, mail merge uses a *master document* and a *data source* to accomplish the task. The master document is the template (although not a template in the Word document sense) that lays out your document and contains text or other items that never change. This might be the sales letter, for example, that you want to send out to all your customers. The master document also contains instructions for inserting data from a data source into each document. The *data source* is your contact list, Excel spreadsheet data, or other file containing the name and address information you want to merge with the document.

The goal of mail merge is simple: to produce many different documents that are personalized to go to many different individuals—without a lot of extra work from you. The process of putting together a mail merge document may seem a bit complicated at first, but it's really just a matter of telling Word where to substitute the different data items. (For example, the *name* goes here and the *address* goes there.) Once you use the mail merge feature a time or two, it will seem fairly intuitive. After you master the basic mail merge process, you can get a little fancier by adding conditional expressions, which enable you to create a mail merge letter for a customer if a certain condition is true.

> **Tip** ✓
>
> There's one change for Microsoft Works users who plan to use their Works database as the data source for Word 2010 mail merge. Now you need to export your data and then create a new data source before importing the information into Word. Word 2010 no longer directly imports Works databases.

It's More than Letters

The mail merge feature can do more than create form letters and address envelopes. You can save the merged documents as a file so that you can edit them or send them by e-mail. You can create almost any type of document by using a specific template or designing the document from scratch. All Word needs is a data document with some data fields in it. You can create mailing labels and address books, awards, parts lists, different versions of exams, and catalogs designed for specific geographical areas or demographic populations. The uses for mail merge are limited only by your creativity, your willingness to experiment with different data fields and Word fields, and your decision as to whether mail merge would be faster than manually creating individual documents.

Setting Conditional Content

Mail merge offers you a flexible way to produce content based on what your customers want to see. You can easily tailor the content according to the data stored in your mailing list. For example, you might offer one promotion to individuals who live in the West Coast region, but offer a different promotion to those who live in the southern United States. If you have an entry in your data file that tracks the region in which the customer lives, you can use that data to control the content of your document. To add this kind of conditional content, you use the IF field, available in the Rules tool in the Mailings tab. You can tell Word to insert one set of content IF the contact lives in the western region or insert a different set of content IF the contact lives in the southern region.

Creating a Form Letter

If the idea of creating a form letter sends a shudder of apprehension down your spine, relax; it's no more difficult than writing a simple note to a co-worker. Once you create the letter, you can customize it by adding the mail merge fields you want—and then it's just a few short steps to the final merge process.

Set Up Your Letter

① Create your letter as you would any other letter, leaving blank any parts that you want to be completed with data from your mailing list. Save the letter.

② On the Mailings tab, click Start Mail Merge in the Start Mail Merge group, and choose Letters from the drop-down menu.

③ Click the Select Recipients button, and specify the type of data you want to use for your mailing list:

- Type **New List** to enter your data in the New Address List dialog box.

- Use Existing List to use data that exists in a file Word can read. To see which type of data sources you can use, open the Files Of Type list in the Select Data Source dialog box, and review the list.

- Select From Outlook Contacts to use data from your Outlook Contacts list.

④ Click Edit Recipient List to display the Mail Merge Recipients dialog box.

⑤ Select or clear check boxes to designate whom you want to include in the mail merge.

⑥ Choose the options you want to apply to the information. Click OK when you've finished.

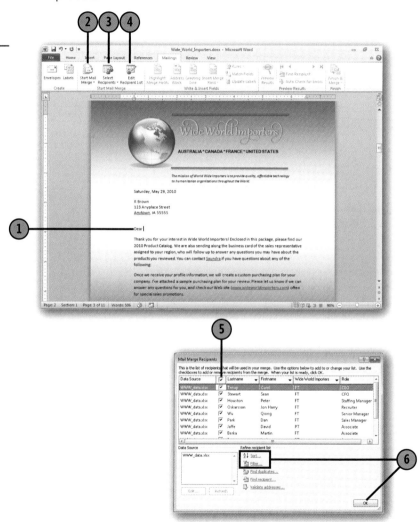

Specify the Data to Be Merged

(1) In your document, click where you want to add information from your data source.

(2) In the Write & Insert Fields group, click the type of information you want to insert.

(3) In the dialog box that appears, specify the options you want and then click OK. Continue adding items to the letter.

(4) Click the Preview Results button to display your data in the document.

(5) Use the buttons to see how your form letters will look when they're merged with the different data records.

(6) Click Edit Recipient List if you see that the form letter you're previewing is addressed to someone you don't want to include in this mailing. In the Mail Merge Recipients dialog box, clear the check box for that individual and click OK.

(7) Click Auto Check For Errors and choose to do a simulated merge to check the document for errors. Correct any errors.

(8) Click Finish & Merge and specify how you want your letters to be completed.

Tip

You can also use the Mail Merge Wizard to step you through the process of using mail merge to prepare a mailing. Click the Start Mail Merge tool in the Start Mail Merge group of the Mailings tab, and choose Step By Step Mail Merge Wizard from the menu to get started.

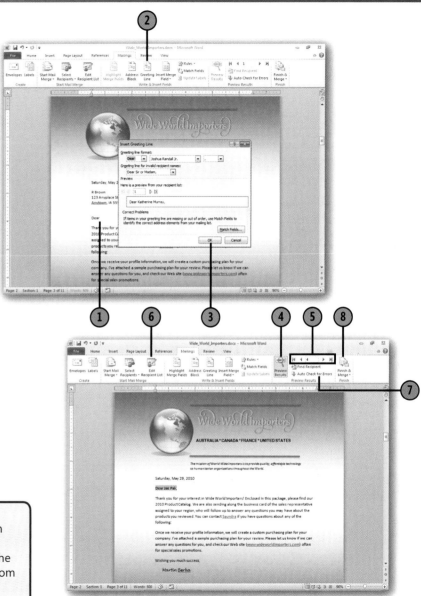

Personalizing a Form Letter

When you use Word's mail merge feature, you aren't limited to simply adding names and addresses. Word includes a number of different fields that enable you to merge the data you need to add in your specific documents. You can also create merge operations that include conditional information so that data is merged only if specific criteria are met.

Include Personalized Information

1. Create your form letter and add your recipient data and a greeting, if necessary.

2. Click where you want to add the personalized information.

3. Click the down arrow on the Insert Merge Field button in the Write & Insert Fields group and select the field you want to insert.

4. Click the Preview Results button and step through some of the records to make sure the field is working correctly.

5. Repeat steps 2 through 4 to insert any other merge fields you want.

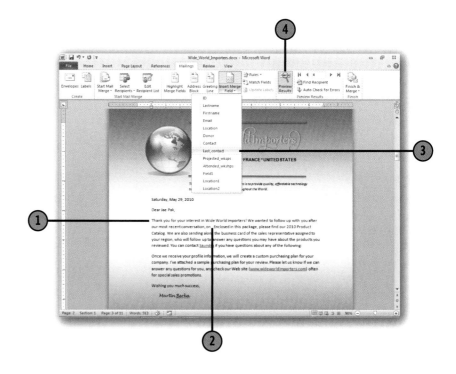

Tip

If you click the Insert Merge Field button instead of the down arrow on the button, the Insert Merge Field dialog box appears. In this dialog box, you can choose to insert address fields that aren't currently part of your data field in case you want to change or modify your data source later.

Tip

Word provides several templates designed for creating form letters and other mail-merged documents. When you open one of these templates, you'll find some fields already inserted into your document.

Add Conditional Content

1 Click where you want to add the conditional information.

2 Click Rules and choose If...Then...Else... from the drop-down list.

3 In the Insert Word Field: IF dialog box, select the field that contains the condition you want to use.

4 Specify how you want to evaluate the condition.

5 Enter the value to be used to evaluate the condition.

6 Enter the text to be inserted if the condition is evaluated as true.

7 Enter the text to be inserted if the condition is evaluated as not true.

8 Click OK.

9 Click Preview Results and step through some of the records to make sure that the field is working correctly. When you're ready, print the merged letters.

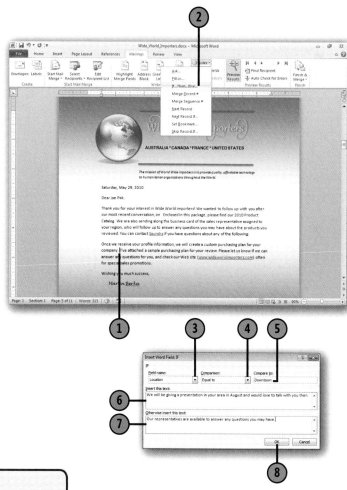

Tip

Use the Fill-In conditional field if you want to be prompted for text each time a record is merged and use the Next Record If field or the Skip Record If field if you want to control which records are merged based on a record in the Recipients database.

8

Adding Special Features for Long Documents

Not all documents are short and simple to create. One of the great things about Microsoft Word 2010 is that it can be as straightforward or as powerful as you need it to be. Although creating basic documents such as memos, letters, and brief reports is a snap, Word also gives you a large variety of tools you can use when you want to create longer, more complex documents such as technical reports, books, dissertations, and more.

Longer documents often call for features that help readers find their way through the text—for example, running heads, footnotes, and bookmarks become important. Likewise, in a longer document, you may also need to add citations and perhaps a table of contents and an index. This section shows you how to add these features—and more—to the long documents you create in Word.

Creating Headers and Footers

Most documents, if they are more than one page in length, include page numbers, either at the top or bottom of the page. In addition to page numbers, long documents usually have some type of identifying text—perhaps the title, section heading, or author's name—at the top or bottom of each page. Typically you'll see the terms *header* and *footer* used to describe these bits of repeating information, but you may also see the term *running head*. Word 2010 includes a special header and footer area on the page that appears when you click at the very top or bottom of the page; and this area brings with it the contextual tools you need to add, edit, and format headers and footers in your document.

Create a Header and Footer

(1) Click the Print Layout icon if necessary.

(2) On the Insert tab, click the Header tool in the Header & Footer group. In the gallery that appears, click your choice.

(3) Click the placeholder field or text, and enter the information you want to appear.

(4) On the Header & Footer Tools Design tab, click the Go To Footer tool in the Navigation group, select the layout and content you want, and type the footer information.

(5) Click the Close Header And Footer button to return to the main part of your document.

> **Tip** ✓
> You can see the headers and footers on your page only in Print Layout view or in Print Preview.

> **Tip** ✓
> You may want to simply type information—such as title or author name—in the header or footer, but you can also add fields that insert your document's properties in the text. For more about this, see "Creating Variable Headers and Footers" on page 178.

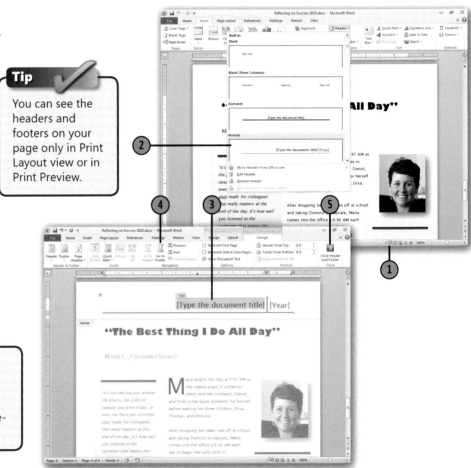

Edit a Header and Footer

1. On the Insert tab, click the Header tool in the Header & Footer group and then click Edit Header in the gallery.

2. If there are items you don't want in the header, delete them and then use any of the items on the Header & Footer Tools Design tab to add content and format the header. Type or add the content you want. Use tabs, paragraph spacing and alignment, and font settings to customize the layout.

3. Click the Go To Footer tool.

4. Add and format the content you want in the footer.

5. Click the Close Header And Footer tool when you've finished.

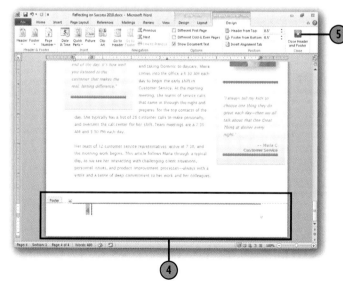

Creating Variable Headers and Footers

When you look through books—like this one—you'll notice that the headers and maybe the footers alternate, depending on which page you're looking at. The header on an even-numbered page looks different from the header on an odd-numbered page. You can set up this design easily in Word by creating different headers and footers that appear on right and left pages.

Create a First-Page Header and Footer

1. Press Ctrl+Home to move to the first page of your document.

2. Click the Insert tab and Different First Page.

3. Create the header, if any, you want to appear on the first page.

4. Click Go To Footer in the Navigation group and create the footer you want, or create a custom footer.

Tip

It's a common practice to omit the header or footer on the first page of a document or the first page of each chapter in a book. If you want to omit the header or footer, leave the first-page header and footer areas blank.

Lets you know the first page header is different from remaining pages

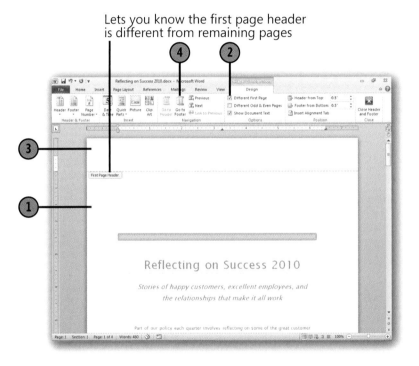

Create Even-Page and Odd-Page Headers and Footers

1. Double-click in the header or footer area, and click Different Odd & Even Pages in the Options group of the Header & Footer Tools Design tab.

2. Add a header or footer to the even-numbered page.

3. Move to an odd-numbered page and create a header and footer.

4. Click in the lower-right corner to reduce the Zoom control to 30 percent so that you can see multiple pages in the document window.

5. Review the headers and footers to ensure that they appear correctly.

Tip

If you are creating a custom header or footer for an even-numbered page, place the text on the left side so that it will appear on the outside edge. For an odd-numbered page, align the text on the right so it will appear along the outside margin of the recto page.

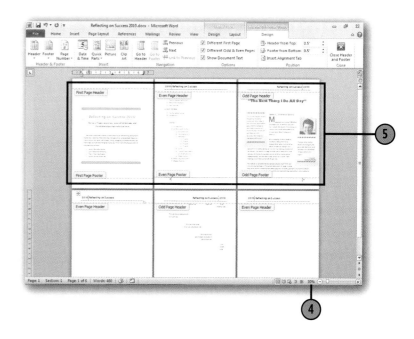

Link and Unlink Headers and Footers

① Click in the header or footer you want to change.

② If Link To Previous is highlighted, the feature is turned on. Click it to turn the link off.

③ If Link To Previous is not highlighted, click to turn the feature on. Now the header or footer on this page will take on the same text and format as the previous header or footer.

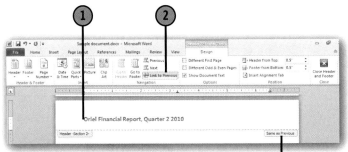

Lets you know the header or footer displays the same text and format as the one on the previous page

Tip ✓

The Link To Previous tool appears only when you are working in the header or footer of a document in which you've created sections.

Organizing Your Information

Tables and lists give you easy ways to present information in a clear, bite-sized format. You can arrange both elements in whatever way you choose to give readers the best possible understanding of your ideas. One way you can help readers get your message is to sort the information and arrange it in alphabetic or numeric order—and Word makes doing that a snap.

Sort a Table

1 Click anywhere in the table, click the Table Tools Layout tab, and click Sort.

2 Specify whether the table will contain a header row (a row that shows the column titles).

3 Specify the title of the column you want to use to sort the table, the type of content in the column, and whether you want the information to be sorted in ascending or descending order.

4 If you want to conduct a second- or third-level sort, enter the criteria.

5 Click OK.

6 Review the results of the sort.

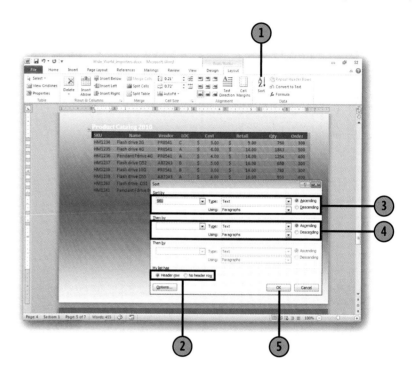

Tip

If you're not happy with the results, either click the Undo tool on the Quick Access Toolbar or conduct another search with different search criteria.

See Also

"Creating a Bulleted or Numbered List" on page 71 for information about creating lists.

Sort a List

① Select the entire list.

② On the Home tab, click Sort in the Paragraph group to display the Sort Text dialog box.

③ Specify whether you want a header row for the list to be included in the selection.

④ To sort a simple list by the first letter, the number, or the date of the paragraph, in the Sort Text dialog box, specify whether you want to sort by paragraphs, the type of information that's in the list, and whether you want the information to be sorted in ascending or descending order. Click OK.

⑤ To sort a more complex list—for example, one that contains columns—click Options to display the Sort Options dialog box, specify the character to be used to separate the columns, and click OK.

⑥ Click OK.

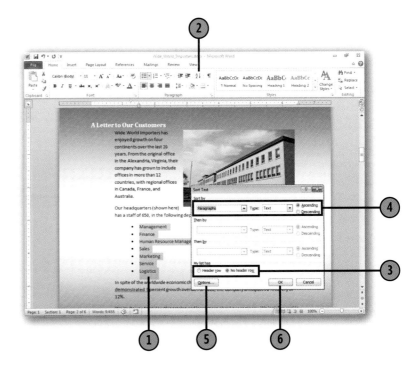

Reorganizing a Document

Outline view may be one of the unsung heroes in Word 2010 when it comes to working with long documents. Using Outline view, you can organize your thoughts, ensure that the overall structure of your document makes sense, and move sections from place to place. You can also change the level of different headings and sections if you like. The only trick to ensuring that your document appears correctly in Outline view is that you need to format the headings and body text using Word styles.

View the Document's Outline

① Click Outline view in the tools in the lower-right corner of the window.

② On the Outlining tab, specify the lowest level of heading to be displayed.

③ Click to expand or collapse the content under the selected heading.

④ Click to change the outline level by promoting it one level or demoting it one level, or to change body text to a heading or a heading to body text.

A minus sign indicates that there's no content under the heading.

An underline indicates that the content under the heading is collapsed and not shown.

A plus sign indicates that there's content under the heading.

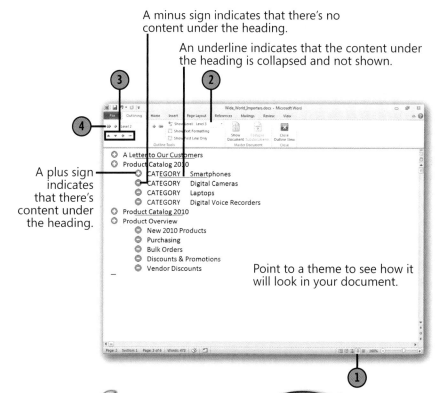

Point to a theme to see how it will look in your document.

Try This!

Drag a topic's plus or minus sign to the left to quickly promote the topic's outline level, to the right to demote it, or to the far right to turn it into body text. Changing the outline level also changes the style that's assigned to that paragraph.

Tip

To quickly expand or collapse a section, double-click the plus sign next to the heading.

See Also

"Applying and Saving Styles" on page 66 for the steps on applying Word's styles to your text.

Move a Paragraph

(1) Expand the outline so the paragraph you want to move and the area into which you want to move it are both displayed.

(2) Click in the paragraph you want to move.

(3) Click to move the paragraph up or down in the document.

Tip

When you select and move a section, all the paragraphs in that section are moved, including those that haven't been expanded and displayed.

Tip

To quickly move a section, click the plus sign next to the heading, and then drag the heading up or down in the document.

Move a Section

1. Click a plus sign to select the section heading and all the content contained under that heading.

2. Drag to move the heading and all its content up or down in the document.

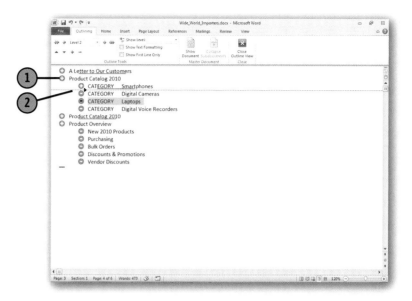

Creating a Master Document

When you are working on a large document that has multiple authors, you may want to create a master document to keep everything organized and help others collaborate effectively. A master document contains *subdocuments,* in which individual authors work to make changes, edit content, and add formatting and illustrations as needed. All the changes are coordinated, so whether you edit documents separately or as part of the master document, all the changes are saved. When the separate documents are incorporated into the master document, you can easily establish common styles and formatting and can develop pagination, cross-references, and a table of contents.

Create the Master Document

1 Start a new document that will be used for the entire master document. Add any introductory text to the master document, save it, and switch to Outline view.

2 On the Outlining tab, click the Show Document button in the Master Document group.

3 Select the text you want to use to create a subdocument and click Create.

4 Move the subdocument to a new area in the document by dragging it to the new location.

5 Insert new text as a subdocument by clicking Insert and choosing the document file from the Insert Subdocument dialog box.

6 Collapse the display of the subdocument by selecting the subdocument section and clicking Collapse Subdocuments in the Master Document group.

7 Open any of the documents separately, and edit and save them. The next time you open the master document, you'll see any editing changes that have been made to these documents.

Expand or collapse topics using the outlining tools.

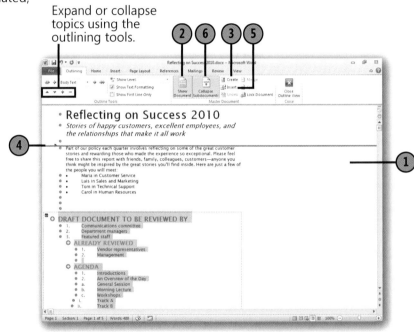

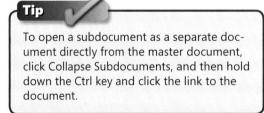

Tip
To open a subdocument as a separate document directly from the master document, click Collapse Subdocuments, and then hold down the Ctrl key and click the link to the document.

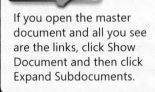

Tip
If you open the master document and all you see are the links, click Show Document and then click Expand Subdocuments.

Inserting a Cover Page

When you're creating a long document, designing a cover page that sets your project apart can help you make a great impression. A cover page might include the title, the authors' names, your department, and a photo or logo, all set in a memorable design. Word 2010 offers a number of cover page templates you can customize to fit the way you want your publication to look.

Insert a Cover Page

(1) Click the Insert tab, click Cover Page in the Pages group, and click the cover page design you want in the gallery that appears.

(2) Switch to Print Layout view if necessary by clicking the view tool in the lower-right corner of the screen and press Ctrl+Home to move to the beginning of your document.

(3) Click in one of the placeholder text boxes and type the information you want to include. Repeat for all the other areas that need to be completed.

(4) You can change the design of the cover page by

- Clicking Cover Page on the Insert tab and choosing another design.

- Clicking Themes on the Page Layout tab and choosing a different theme.

- Adding a picture, a drawing, fields, text, or other items to customize the page.

- Changing the color of the page background.

- Clicking Cover Page again, and choosing Remove Current Cover Page.

(5) Save your document.

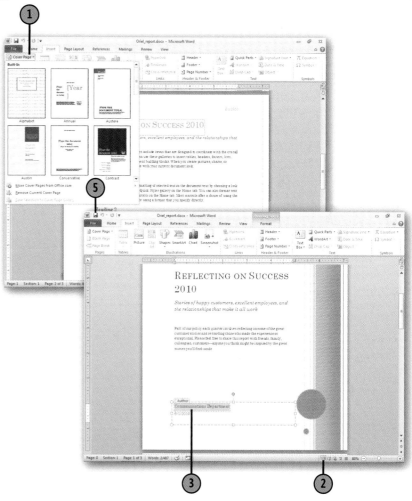

Creating Footnotes and Endnotes

When you are working with long documents, you may need to add footnotes or endnotes to the text to provide additional information about resources you've used. Footnotes add the notes along the bottom of the page, and endnotes present all your notes at the end of the document or section. Word numbers the footnotes in one number series and the endnotes in a different series or format. If you add or delete a footnote or an endnote, Word automatically renumbers the appropriate series. Word also estimates how much space is required for the footnote and, if a footnote is too long for the page, automatically continues it on the next page.

Insert a Footnote or an Endnote

1 Click the References tab, with the insertion point located where you want the footnote or endnote reference mark to appear in your document; click Insert Footnote for a footnote or Insert Endnote in the Footnotes group for an endnote.

2 Type your footnote or endnote text.

3 Double-click the footnote or endnote number to return to the place in your document where you inserted the footnote.

Tip

You enter footnote/endnote text directly on the page in Print Layout view. In Web Layout, Outline, and Draft views, you enter the text in a Footnote pane that appears at the bottom of the window when you insert the mark.

Change the Reference Mark

① On the References tab, click the Footnote & Endnote tool in the Footnotes group.

② Specify where you want the footnotes or endnotes to appear, and click the numbering series you want.

③ Click to display the Symbol dialog box, choose a symbol for the footnote or endnote mark, and click OK.

④ Click Apply.

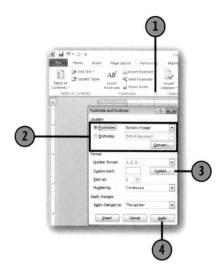

Creating a Table of Contents

Word also includes a table of contents feature that creates a table based on the styles you've assigned to the headings in your document and displays the current page numbers so your readers can easily find the section they're looking for. The table of contents is inserted as a field in a content control, so after you've created the table, you can change its layout by choosing a different design. You can also update the table if you change the content of your document.

Set the Outline Text

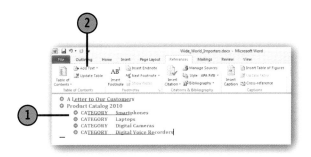

1. Click Outline view in the lower-right corner of the screen and scroll through the document, verifying that any paragraph you want to appear in the table of contents has a style that uses the appropriate level 1, level 2, or level 3 outline level.

2. If you want to include or exclude a paragraph but don't want to change its style, click the Add Text tool on the References tab and click the outline level you want to apply.

(continued on next page)

Tip

If a paragraph you want to include in the table of contents doesn't have a style with the appropriate outline level, click in the paragraph and apply the appropriate style before you choose the Table of Contents command.

Set the Outline Text *(continued)*

③ Switch to Print Layout view and click in the document where you want the table of contents to appear.

④ On the References tab, click the Table Of Contents tool in the Table Of Contents group, and select the style and type of table of contents you want to insert.

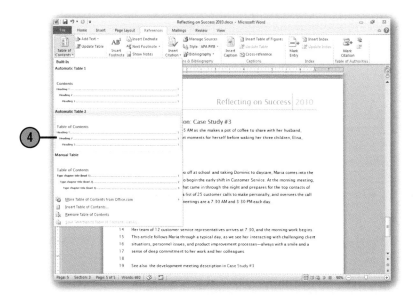

Tip ✓

To update the table of contents after you've made changes to your document, click the Update Table tool on the References tab.

See Also ➤

"Applying and Saving Styles" on page 66 for information about assigning styles to your text.

Creating an Index

Indexing can be fun. If you're a word person and you like thinking of the many ways a person might be looking for something in your document, you'll probably enjoy the puzzle creating an index presents. Word makes the process straightforward by automating the steps. When you mark an item to be included in your index, Word places a hidden-text tag next to the item, so no matter how the page numbers change, the index is kept current. Your index can include multiple levels, cross-references, and even a range of pages when an indexed item extends beyond a single page.

Tag the Entries

① Click the References tab and click the Mark Entry tool in the Index group to display the Mark Index Entry dialog box.

② In your document, select the text you want to index.

③ Click the Mark Index Entry dialog box to make it active. The text you selected appears in the Main Entry box.

④ Type any subentries. To specify more than one level of subentry, separate subentry levels with colons.

⑤ Specify options as follows:

- Click Cross-Reference and type the topic to be cross-referenced.

- Click Current Page to list the page number next to the entry.

- Click Page Range and select the bookmark that marks the entire text of the entry. The text must be bookmarked before it can be included as an entry.

⑥ Click in the document, select your next index entry, and repeat steps 3 through 5.

⑦ When you've finished, click Close and save the document.

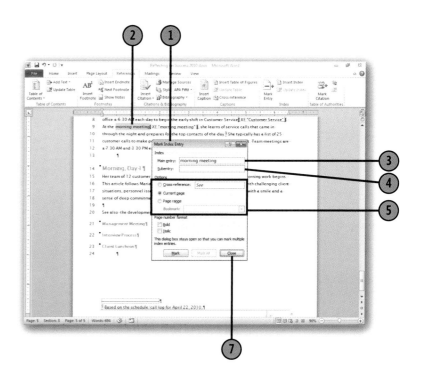

Compile the Index

1 Press Ctrl+End to move to the end of the document.

2 Click the References tab and click Insert Index to display the Index dialog box.

3 Select the type of index you want.

4 Specify the number of columns the index will occupy on the page.

5 Clear this check box to have the page numbers placed immediately next to the entry, or select the check box to have Word insert a tab and align the page numbers to the right edge of each column. If you selected the check box, choose the type of tab leader you want between the index entry and the page number.

6 Specify the format you want for the index. If you chose From Template, click the Modify button to change the styles used for the index.

7 Click OK.

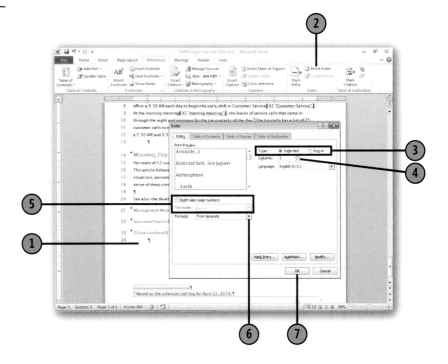

Try This!

To cross-reference a related entry but still include a page number, tag the entry twice—once using *"See also"* in the Cross-Reference box and again with the Current Page option selected.

Tip

The Mark All button in the Mark Index Entry dialog box finds every instance in your document of the text you've selected and marks each instance with the tag information you entered in the dialog box. The AutoMark button in the Index dialog box lets you specify a document that contains a list of items you want Word to mark automatically for your index. If you use either of these automated techniques, you'll need to go through your document and carefully verify these index entries.

Sharing, Co-Authoring, and Finalizing Your Document

In today's rapidly growing worldwide marketplace, being able to share and work collaboratively on documents is more important than ever. Microsoft Word 2010 includes a big new co-authoring feature that enables you to actually work on your document alongside other authors. After you've saved the file to Microsoft SharePoint Workspace or Windows Live SkyDrive, you can open, edit, and save the file while seeing what others are doing in the file at the same time.

Word also includes a number of features that help you keep track of all the edits being made so that you can easily finalize the document after all the hard work is done. Using Track Changes, you can see the changes made by each reviewer, and then you can choose whether to accept or reject the changes that were made. When you've reviewed all the reviews and accepted or rejected the changes, you can then merge all the disparate pieces into one final document. When you're ready to finalize your document, Word provides tools to help you make sure protections are in place and you're sharing just what you intend to share.

Working Collaboratively with Word 2010

With Word 2010, you can be more flexible and collaborative than ever. New tools enable you to work literally anywhere you have Internet access, share your files easily with friends and colleagues, and even co-author your files live with others while you're all working in the document at the same time.

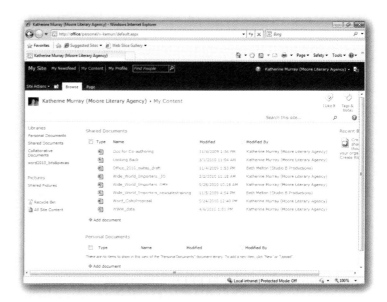

Word 2010 Web App

The Word 2010 Web App gives you the same familiar Word interface—complete with the ribbon and all your favorite tools—available in your Web browser. First, you save your file to Windows Live SkyDrive (a free service that is part of Windows Live) or Microsoft SharePoint Workspace 2010 (which is part of Microsoft Office 2010 Professional Plus), and then you can open, edit, share, and save your file normally in your favorite Web browser.

Microsoft SharePoint Workspace 2010

Microsoft SharePoint Workspace 2010 is a collaboration tool that is part of Microsoft Office 2010 Professional Plus. This server-based tool enables colleagues to create document libraries, chat online, co-author documents, download files from the server, and much more.

Windows Live SkyDrive

Windows Live SkyDrive (*www.skydrive.live.com*) is a free file storage and sharing service that is part of Microsoft's Windows Live services. This type of online file management service is often referred to as *cloud computing* and is quickly becoming an energy-efficient, convenient way for individual users and businesses to back up and manage files while accessing them from any point they have Web or smartphone access. All you need to create a Windows Live SkyDrive account is a Windows Live ID, and Word 2010 walks you through the process the first time you attempt to save a file to Windows Live SkyDrive.

Microsoft Office 2010 Upload Center

The Microsoft Office 2010 Upload Center is a tool that is available as part of Office 2010, designed to manage your file transfers when you need to synchronize files with a server. In most cases, the Upload Center handles transfers transparently, but you can display the Upload Center to check recent transfers, scheduled transfers, and more.

Using the Word 2010 Web App

Word 2010 makes it easy for you to continue your work anywhere you have Web access by using the Word 2010 Web App. Now you can save your file to Windows Live SkyDrive and open it in a Web browser and continue working on it—adding content and formatting content; revising and updating your text and images, diagrams, and charts. You can also use the Word 2010 Web App with Microsoft SharePoint Workspace 2010, which is available with Microsoft Office 2010 Professional Plus.

Save Your Document to a Shared Space

① Open the document you want to save online.

② Click File and click Save & Send.

③ Click Save To Web.

④ Click one of the folders shown.

   Or

⑤ Click New to sign in and create a new online folder.

⑥ Click Save As.

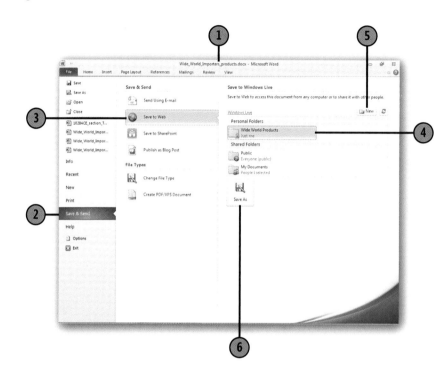

Open a Document in Windows Live SkyDrive

(1) Open your Web browser and log in to your Windows Live account.

(2) Click Office at the top of the window.

(3) Click the document you want to open.

(4) Click Edit In Browser.

(5) Use the tools in the ribbon to make changes as needed.

(6) Click Save to save your changes in the online file.

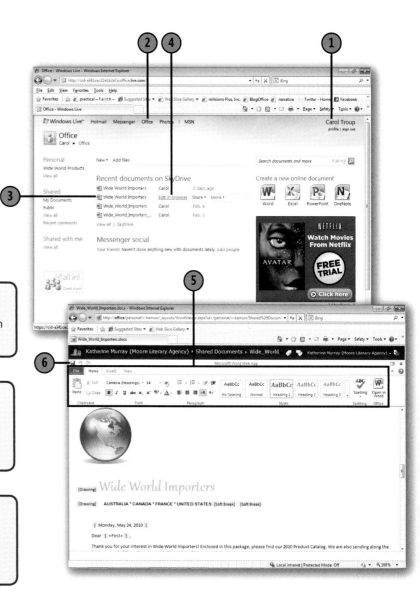

Tip

You can also open a document in Word 2010, which opens the file on your computer and then synchronizes your changes with the version on the server when you save the file.

Tip

You can add more files to your Windows Live SkyDrive account by clicking Add Files and then dragging and dropping files to the upload space or clicking Select Files From Your Computer and choosing the files you want to add.

Tip

Windows Live also includes a Windows Live Sign-In Assistant that you can install so that you don't need to sign in to Windows Live in the future when you save a document to your online account.

Co-Authoring a Document

If you are working with someone else preparing a document—perhaps a newsletter for a neighborhood association or a brochure for a nonprofit group—you need to be able to add your content and make changes, and then review what the other person has done as well. Now in Word 2010 you can both work in the file at the same time if you like. As each person edits the file, the section being edited is locked so the other person can't change that section. Both you and your co-author can see the changes being made in real time and contact each other online using the presence features available through Office Communicator.

Set Co-Author Permissions

1. Log in to your Windows Live SkyDrive account.

2. Click the file you want to share.

3. Click Share and click Edit Permissions. In the next window, click My Documents and then click the link in the Shared With field.

(continued on next page)

Set Co-Author Permissions *(continued)*

④ Click Edit Permissions again.

⑤ Type your co-author's e-mail address and press Enter.

⑥ Choose the level of permission you want your co-author to have.

⑦ Click Save.

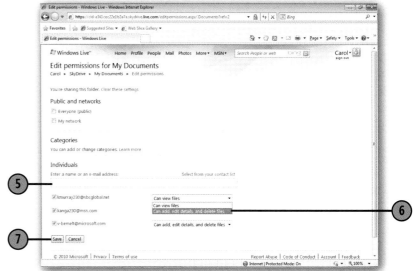

Work with a Co-Author

(1) Open the file you want to edit.

(2) An alert lets you know when a co-author begins working in the file.

(3) Click the indicator in the status bar to see who else is working in the file.

(4) Edit the file normally, adding content and making changes as needed.

(5) Click Save to save the file.

Tip

If you want to block a co-author from working on a section of a shared file, select the text you want to protect and click the Review tab; then click Block Authors in the Protect group.

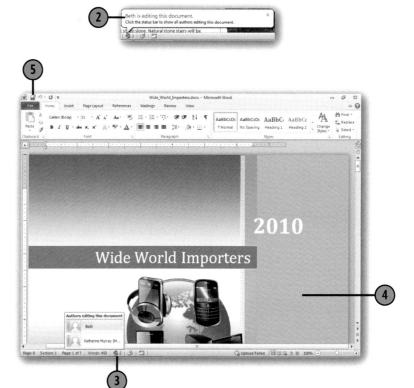

Contacting Co-Authors

When you are working simultaneously in a file with a co-author, you can contact your co-author by e-mail, instant message, or phone to ask questions about the file, discuss possibilities, or just generally talk through your plans for the edits.

Contact a Co-Author

1. Open the document to be reviewed.

2. Click the indicator in the status bar and click the author's name.

3. Click an icon to choose the action you want to perform:

   - Send an e-mail message to the author

   - Start an instant messaging conversation

   - Make a phone call

   - Schedule a meeting

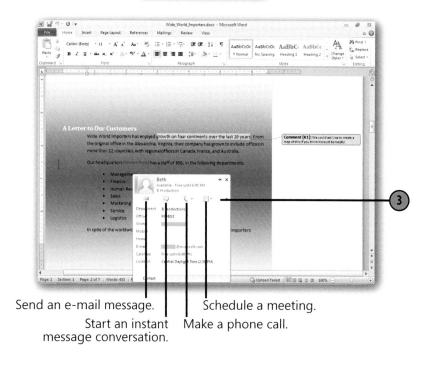

Send an e-mail message.

Start an instant message conversation.

Make a phone call.

Schedule a meeting.

Reviewing Shared File Information

When you are working with a shared file, you can use the File tab to display information about file status, co-authors, and version information. Begin by clicking File to display Backstage view. The Info tab provides file properties as well as information related to the sharing of the file.

Get File Information

① While you're working with the shared document, click File.

② In the Info tab, review information in the center panel.

③ Click a co-author if you want to send a message.

④ Click to send an e-mail message or start an instant messaging conversation.

⑤ Review version information.

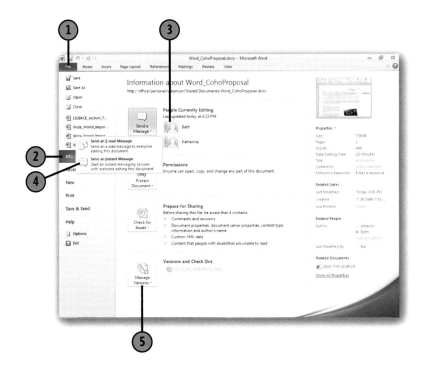

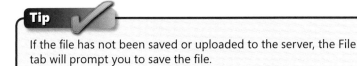

Tip

If the file has not been saved or uploaded to the server, the File tab will prompt you to save the file.

Update a Shared File

(1) When prompted, click Save.

(2) You can also click Updates Available to upload changes to the server.

Working with Revision Marks

When you are working in a document that you plan to share with others, you can turn on Track Changes so that you can easily see where others make changes in the file. When Track Changes is turned on, Word marks all additions, deletions, moves, and formatting changes. When you're reviewing the edited document, you can accept or reject any change or comment, view the changes made by individual reviewers, and even view the document as it was before any of the changes were made. You can also view the document as it would look if you accepted all the changes.

Review a Document

1. Open the document to be reviewed.

2. On the Review tab, click Track Changes in the Tracking group if it isn't already selected.

3. Click Final Showing Markup in the Tracking group to see your changes.

4. Edit the content as usual. You can see the changes in the text.

5. To insert a comment, select the text you want to comment on and click New Comment.

6. Type your comment in the balloon that appears.

7. Choose Final view, review the document for any errors, and then save and close it.

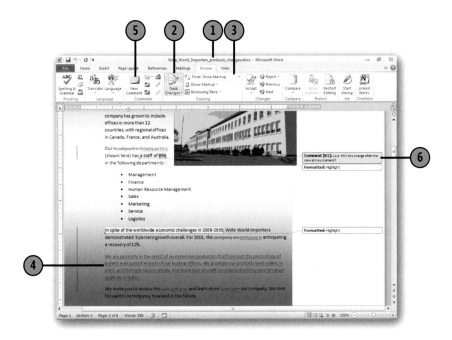

Tip

In Draft view, all the changes are marked in the document, and any descriptions and comments are displayed in the Reviewing pane on the left side or at the bottom of the window. When you're working in Page Layout view, click the Review tab and click Show Markup in the Tracking group to display the list. Point to Balloons to display the options that control how content changes appear in the document.

Review a Document with Tracked Changes

① Open a document that has been reviewed and edited. If it's marked as Read-Only, save it using a different name.

② On the Review tab, click Track Changes in the Tracking group, if it's selected, to turn it off.

③ Switch to Final Showing Markup view if it isn't already selected.

④ Click Final: Show Markup, and specify the types of changes you want to be displayed. If you don't want to see the markup from every reviewer, specify which reviewers' changes you do want to see.

⑤ Click Next to locate a change. Click Accept to include the change or click Reject to delete the change. Continue choosing Accept or Reject to review and incorporate changes. To accept all the changes, click the down arrow on the Accept tool and choose Accept All Changes In Document from the drop-down menu. To reject all changes, click the down arrow on the Reject tool and choose Reject All Changes In Document.

⑥ When you've finished, switch to Final: Show Markup view, review the document for any errors, and then save and close it.

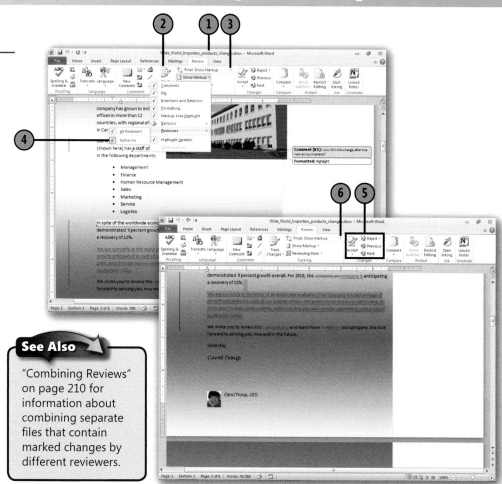

See Also

"Combining Reviews" on page 210 for information about combining separate files that contain marked changes by different reviewers.

Tip

To highlight text without adding a comment, click the Highlight tool on the Home tab and drag the mouse pointer over the content you want to highlight.

See Also

"Comparing Changes in a Document" on the next page for information about comparing two versions of the same document and marking the changes.

Comparing Changes in a Document

If you have two versions of the same document, and changes have been made but not marked in one of them, how do you know what changes were made? Using Word's Compare feature, you can compare the original with the revised document and have Word mark all the changes.

Prepare to Compare

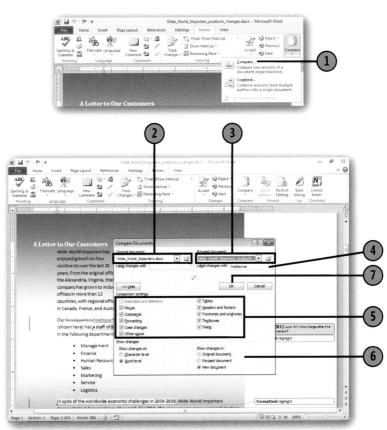

(1) On the Review tab, click Compare in the Compare group and, in the gallery that appears, choose Compare to display the Compare Documents dialog box.

(2) Specify the original document by clicking either the down arrow to see a list of recently used documents or the Browse button to locate and select the document.

(3) Specify the revised document.

(4) If you want to change the name assigned to a reviewer's changes—to Reviewer 1, for example—enter the new name.

(5) If the More button is displayed, click it to show the options for the comparison. (When the More button has been clicked, it's replaced by the Less button.) Clear the check boxes for any items you don't want to be marked and select the check boxes for the items you do want to be marked.

(6) Specify how and where you want the changes to be shown.

(7) Click OK.

Tip

You can use this method of comparison to create legal black-lining in contracts or agreements so that each party can see how the original document was revised.

Review the Changes

① Click the Reviewing Pane tool to show or hide the Reviewing pane. Click the down arrow at the right of the Reviewing Pane tool to change the location of the Reviewing pane.

② Scroll through the main document, noting the changes. As you scroll, the source documents are simultaneously scrolled so that the same parts of the documents are shown in all windows.

③ Save the main document with the marked changes.

④ Review the main document, using the same methods you normally use when you're reviewing any document that contains marked changes.

③ The Reviewing pane **①** The main document

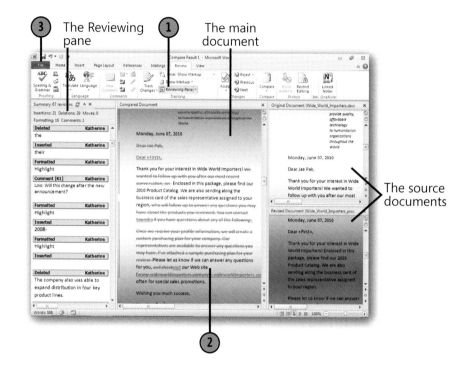

The source documents

Combining Reviews

When co-authoring isn't an option, you may need to send a document out for review. This means you're likely to get back several separately reviewed and/or edited copies of the document. How do you combine all those separate changes into one document? If others used Word's Track Changes feature, you can combine all their changes and comments by merging the separate documents into a single document so that you can easily create a final version.

Merge the Documents

① Click Compare in the Compare group of the Review tab and click Combine.

② Specify the document that contains the first set of reviews you want to use.

③ Select the document with the second set of reviews.

④ Click the More button if you want to modify which changes are displayed and in which document. (When the More button has been clicked, it's replaced by the Less button.) Select the check boxes for the items you want to be marked as changed.

⑤ Specify whether you want each character or each word change to be noted and specify where you want the changes to be shown.

⑥ Click OK and then save the merged document.

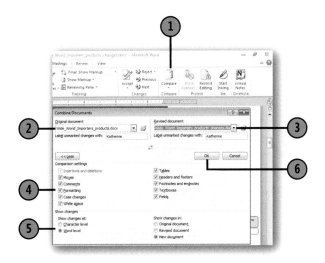

When you combine two documents, you can include the formatting changes from only one of the documents. It's a good idea, therefore, to clear the Formatting check box if you want to keep the formatting changes marked in the original document; otherwise, you can end up with only the formatting changes made in the revised document.

Viewing Documents Side by Side

When you want to look at two documents simultaneously to compare their content, Word will place the documents in adjacent windows. If the documents are similar enough, you can have Word scroll through both of them at the same time or you can scroll through the documents one at a time.

View the Documents

1 Open the two documents you want to view and compare.

2 On the View tab, in one document, click the View Side By Side tool in the Windows group.

3 If a dialog box appears and asks you which document you want to view, select the document you want, and click OK.

4 If you don't want the documents to scroll together, on the View tab, click the Window tool to expand the window section (if it's collapsed), and click Synchronous Scrolling to turn off the scrolling. Click Synchronous Scrolling again to resume the coordinated scrolling.

5 Scroll through the documents. When you've finished, click the Window tool again, and click the View Side By Side button to turn off that view.

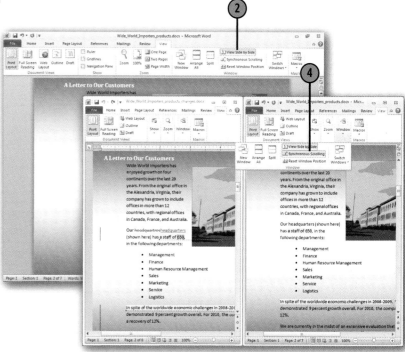

Tip
If you want to see two different parts of the same document, click the Windows Split bar at the top of the vertical scrollbar downward in the document. This splits the screen so that you can scroll to just the area of the document you'd like to see.

Tip
To review more than two documents at one time, open all the documents you want to review and close any that you don't want to include in your review. In any one of the open documents, click Arrange All on the View tab.

Tip
If the two windows don't start at the same part of the document when you start scrolling through them, turn off Synchronous Scrolling, scroll through one window until it displays the same top line as the other window, and turn Synchronous Scrolling back on.

Finalizing Your Document

If you've ever released what you thought was the final version of a document, only to find that there were still changes marked on it or that it contained information you didn't want others to see, you know that you don't want to do that again! And if you've ever released a document whose wording made you cringe because someone had edited it without your permission, you don't want that to happen again, either. Fortunately, Word provides tools to help you ensure that your document is really ready to share before you share it.

Prepare Your Document

① Click File, and in the Info tab, click Check For Issues.

② Click Inspect Document.

(continued on next page)

Tip

If you want to keep others from changing the file, click the File tab and click Protect Document in the Info tab. Choose Mark As Final. Click OK to confirm your choice.

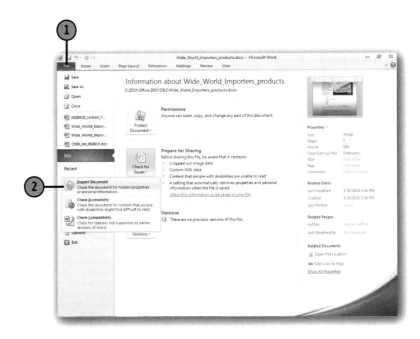

Prepare Your Document *(continued)*

③ Clear the check boxes for the items you want to keep in the document and select the check boxes for the items you don't want to appear in the document.

④ Click Inspect.

⑤ In the Document Inspector dialog box, click the Remove All button for each type of item you want to remove.

⑥ Click Reinspect if you want to recheck the document. Close the dialog box when you're finished.

⑦ Close and distribute the document.

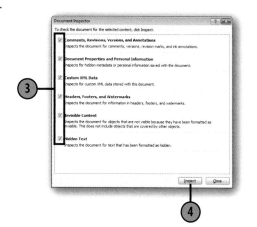
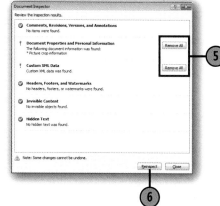

See Also

"Password Protecting a File" on page 231 for information about using additional security settings to prevent changes to your document.

Tip

If you change your mind about a finalized document, you can enable editing again by clicking the File tab and choosing Protect Document in the info tab again; then click Mark As Final a second time to turn off the feature.

10

Customizing and Securing Word

One of the great things about Microsoft Word 2010 is that not only does it pack a lot of power into the various features and tools at your fingertips, but it also allows you to customize those tools so you have just what you want nearby when you want it. You can easily customize the ribbon by adding tabs, tab groups, and tools; you can customize the Quick Access Toolbar by changing the tools it displays and changing where in the document window it appears. What's more, you can change other preferences, such as the way the screen looks, the way your files are saved, and much more.

Another important story in Word 2010 is the enhanced security that occurs largely without your even noticing it. Behind the scenes, Word 2010 is working to ensure that the files you receive and open have been checked—thoroughly—for any possible risk. You can set the types of files you want to be blocked in your version of Word and tell the program when you want Protected View to intervene and safeguard your files and when it's okay to open them directly. These security features—and more—are the topic of this section.

Customizing the Ribbon

You probably remember all the excitement around the introduction of the ribbon, which was offered for the first time with Office 2007. Some people were thrilled, others were dismayed, and most Word users simply figured out how to master the interface and gradually grew to like it. Word 2010 includes a new feature that is huge to Word users who want to have within clicking distance the tools they use most often. Now you can customize the ribbon to include tabs you create. And you can add your own groups and tools to those tabs in whatever order makes sense to you.

Create and Rename a New Tab

1. Click the File tab to display Backstage view.

2. Click Options.

(continued on next page)

Tip

By default a new group is created when you add a new tab. You can add additional groups to the tab by clicking New Group at the bottom of the Customize The Ribbon list.

Create and Rename a New Tab *(continued)*

③ Click Customize Ribbon.

④ Click New Tab.

⑤ Click the new tab.

⑥ Click Rename.

⑦ Type a new name for the tab and click OK.

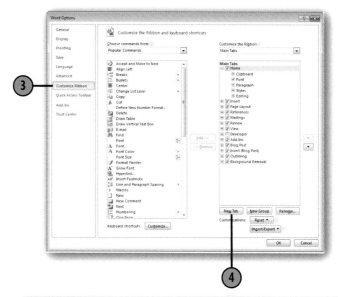

Tip

You can move the group you create up or down through the tabs shown by clicking the Move Down or Move Up buttons.

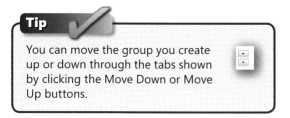

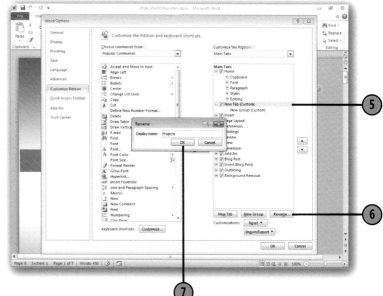

Rename and Add Tools to the Group

① Click the new group that was created automatically.

② Click Rename.

③ Type a name for the group and click OK.

(continued on next page)

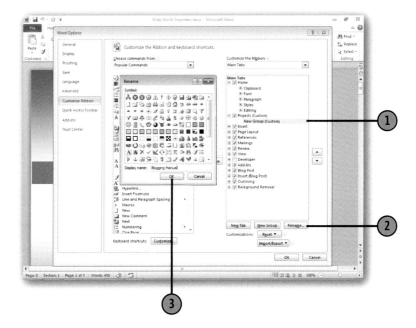

Tip ✔

If you don't see the tools you want in the Popular Commands list, click the Choose Commands From arrow, and choose All Commands. Scroll through the list to find the tool you want, click it, and click Add.

Rename and Add Tools to the Group *(continued)*

④ In the Choose Commands From list, click the tool you want to add to the group.

⑤ Click Add.

⑥ Repeat Steps 4 and 5 as needed until you have added all the tools you want.

⑦ Click OK.

Tip

If you use more than one computer and want to use your customized ribbon on another machine, click the Import/Export button in the lower-right corner of the Customize Ribbon dialog box. Choose Export All Customizations to create a file you can add to other computers. When you move the file to the new computer, use Import Customization File to import your changed ribbon settings.

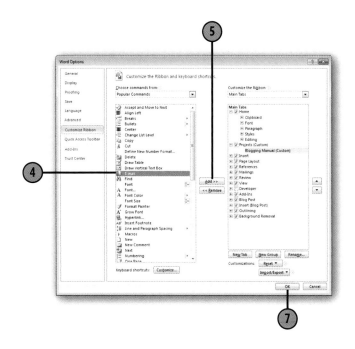

Tip

In addition to selecting the tool and clicking Add, you can add a new tool to the group by simply dragging it from one list to another.

Customizing the Quick Access Toolbar

The Quick Access Toolbar makes it easy for you to have the tools you want to access quickly nearby no matter which Word tabs you may be using. If you put so many items on the Quick Access Toolbar that it becomes too big to fit on the title bar, you can move it to its own line.

Add or Remove Items Common to the Quick Access Toolbar

1 Click the down arrow at the right of the Quick Access Toolbar.

2 On the Customize Quick Access Toolbar menu, click any checked items that you want to remove from the toolbar.

3 Click any unchecked items that you want to add to the toolbar.

4 Right-click any item anywhere on the ribbon that you want to add to the toolbar, and choose Add To Quick Access Toolbar from the shortcut menu.

5 If the toolbar becomes too large to fit on the title bar or if you want to change the location of the bar, click the down arrow at the right of the toolbar and click Show Below The Ribbon on the menu.

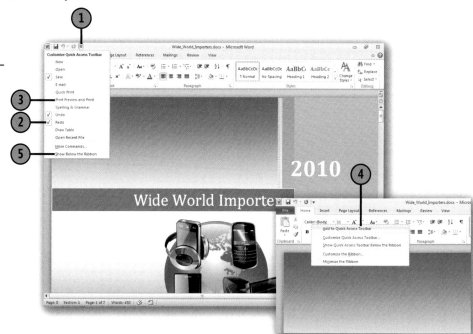

> **Tip**
>
> You can return the Quick Access Toolbar to its spot above the ribbon by clicking the Quick Access Toolbar arrow and choosing Show Above The Ribbon.

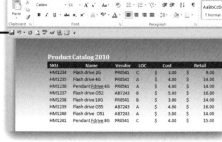

The Quick Access toolbar on its own line below the ribbon

Control the Customization

① Click the Quick Access Toolbar arrow and click More Commands to display the Word Options dialog box with the Customize Ribbon category selected in the left pane.

② Specify the category of commands you want to select from.

③ Click a command you want to add to the toolbar.

④ Click Add.

⑤ To remove a command you don't use, select it and click Remove.

⑥ To change the order in which commands will appear on the toolbar, click a command and use the up or down arrow to move the command.

⑦ Repeat steps 3 through 7 to make any further customizations to the Quick Access Toolbar; click OK when you've finished.

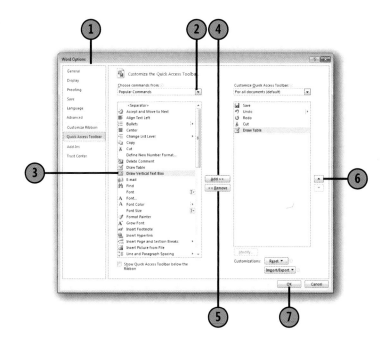

Tip

You're not limited to "standard" Word commands. You can include styles, fonts, and macros on the toolbar.

Tip

When you change the Quick Access Toolbar, the changes you make appear in the toolbar in all your documents. If you want to use that version of the toolbar in the current document only, display the Word Options dialog box, click Quick Access Toolbar, and click the Customize Quick Access Toolbar arrow and choose the name of your current document. Click OK to save your changes.

Customizing the Work Area

The work area is where you create, edit, format, and fine-tune the documents you create in Word 2010, so you may want to customize it to fit your own preferences. You can show or hide items on the status bar, set the ribbon to appear only when you need to use it, change the overall color scheme for the window, and so on.

Show or Hide Items on the Status Bar

1. Right-click anywhere on the status bar.

2. Review the information on the Customize Status Bar menu.

3. To show an item that isn't currently displayed on the status bar, click the item.

4. To hide an item that's currently displayed, click the item.

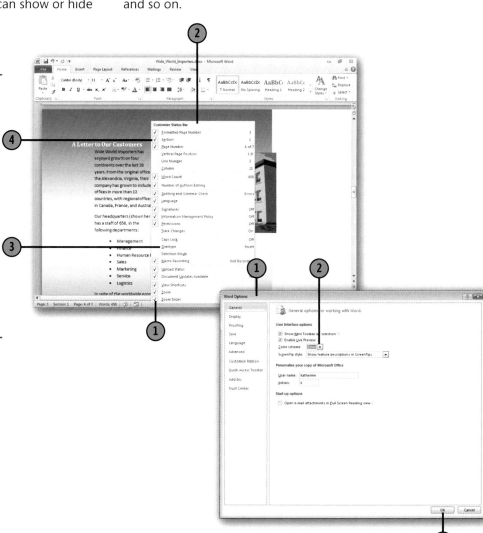

Change the Color Scheme

1. Click the File tab and click Options to display the Word Options dialog box.

2. In the General tab, click Color Scheme and click the color you want.

3. Click OK.

Show or Minimize the Ribbon

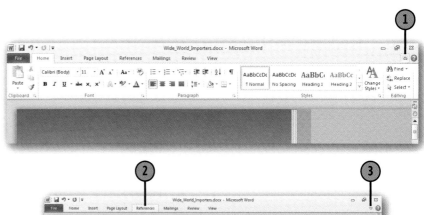

(1) Click the Minimize The ribbon button at the top right of the ribbon.

(2) Display the ribbon by clicking the tab you want. Click a tab when you want to display the ribbon and choose the tool you want. The ribbon is then hidden again.

(3) To redisplay the ribbon, click Maximize The Ribbon.

Try This!

With the ribbon displayed, double-click the active tab to minimize the ribbon, and then click any tab to display the ribbon temporarily. Click in your document to minimize the ribbon again. Double-click the active tab to redisplay the ribbon. Press Ctrl+F1 to hide the ribbon, and press Ctrl+F1 again to always display the ribbon.

Changing the Location and Type of Saved Files

If you want to save your documents in specific folders, you can have Word change the places your files are saved by default. You set file locations and formats using the Word Options dialog box. What's more, you can choose to save your Word files in a previous version if you like, in case you work with peers and friends who are using a previous version of Word. (Note, however, that if you work in a version of Word prior to 2007, many of the new features—including artistic effects, collaborative tools, and more—won't be available in the earlier format.)

Change the File Locations and Formats

1. Click the File tab, click Options and click Advanced. Scroll down to the General area and click the File Locations button to display the File Locations dialog box.

2. Click the item whose location you want to change.

3. Click Modify, and, in the Modify Location dialog box, locate and select the folder that you're designating as the new location; click OK.

4. Specify the location for any other file types and click OK when you've finished.

5. Click the Save category.

6. Select the default format in which you want to save your documents.

7. Click OK to close the Word Options dialog box.

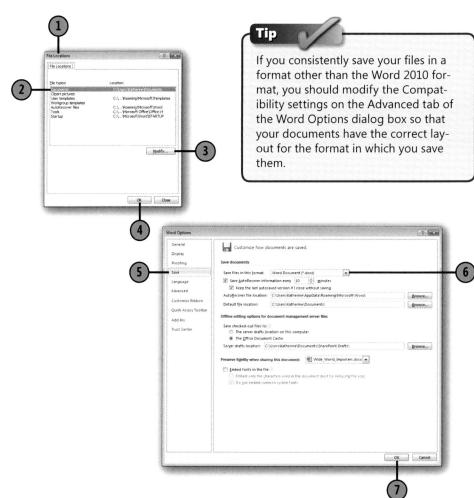

Tip

If you consistently save your files in a format other than the Word 2010 format, you should modify the Compatibility settings on the Advanced tab of the Word Options dialog box so that your documents have the correct layout for the format in which you save them.

Customizing Your Spelling Dictionaries

Word 2010 enables you to use one or more dictionaries to check your spelling. When there's a word in your document that's correct but that Word doesn't recognize—a name, an address, or an unfamiliar technical or scientific term, for example—you can tell Word to add that word to your custom dictionary. If you already have a custom dictionary that

includes many of the words you want Word to recognize as correct, you can add that dictionary to the list of dictionaries that Word is using. Now in Word 2010 you can also choose a dictionary in another language if you are translating or editing in a language other than English.

Add a Dictionary

① Click the File tab and click Options to display the Word Options dialog box.

② Click Proofing.

③ Click the Custom Dictionaries button to display the Custom Dictionaries dialog box.

④ If you have an existing dictionary that you want to use, click Add; in the Add Custom Dictionary dialog box that appears, locate the dictionary file. Click Open.

⑤ To create a dictionary by adding entries, click New, use the Create Custom Dictionary dialog box to name the dictionary file, and click Save.

⑥ To add or delete words in a dictionary, select the dictionary, and click Edit Word List.

⑦ Click Add and type a word, or select a word you want to remove and click Delete.

⑧ Click OK.

⑨ Verify that the dictionaries you want to use are checked and those you don't want to use aren't checked.

⑩ Click OK.

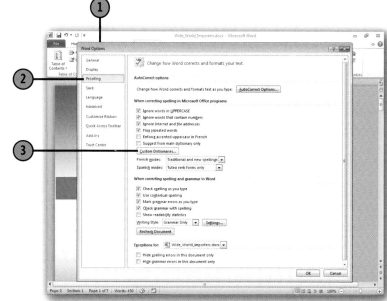

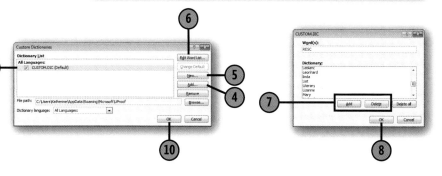

Creating a Macro

You can automate procedures you follow often by creating a macro to record the keystrokes and menu selections and then playing them back by pressing a single key combination. For example, you could create a macro by recording the replacement of a phrase and/or a style using the Replace command. Then you can run that macro to modify other documents. Regardless of the complexity of your macro, you can run it as though it were a single Word command.

Create a Macro

1. Click the View tab, click the Macros arrow in the Macros group, and choose Record Macro to display the Record Macro dialog box.

2. Type a name for the macro. (The name must begin with a letter and can't contain any spaces or symbols.)

3. Choose whether you want to assign the macro to a button or the keyboard.

4. Specify where you want to store the macro and type a description.

5. Click OK.

6. Execute the series of actions you want to record as a macro, using your keyboard to select text and to move the insertion point. (Note that other than when you click a command, most mouse actions aren't recorded.)

7. When you've completed the series of actions, click the Macros arrow again and choose Stop Recording.

8. Click Macros to display the Macros dialog box, select the macro you just recorded and click Run to make sure the macro performs correctly.

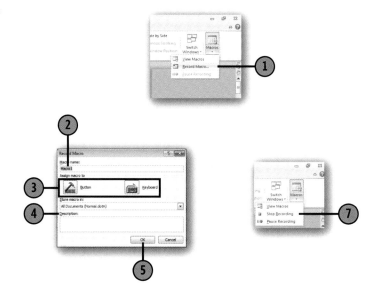

Tip

For the greatest control in creating and modifying macros, add the Developer tab to the ribbon by clicking the File tab, clicking Options, clicking Customize Ribbon, and clicking the Developer tab check box in the list on the right. Click OK to save your changes.

Understanding Security in Office 2010

Today you just can't be too careful about the files you accept and download from the Internet. Every computer user needs some sort of antivirus program that scans incoming files for potential threats and keeps your computer safe from attack. Word 2010 includes improved security features that evaluate files before you open them and then prompting you if something unrecognized is found.

One area developers found vulnerable to attack occurs when you open a file saved in a previous version of Word. To safeguard this process, Word now includes a security check that goes on behind the scenes when you open a new document. The file must pass a series of checks—called a file validation process—before it is considered a safe file. If Word 2010 finds anything suspicious, the document is displayed in Protected View.

Word 2010 shows you that a file is in Protected View by displaying a message bar across the top of the work area. If you know the sender of the file or are certain the file is safe, you can click Enable Editing to remove the protection and edit the file normally. You can change which files Word 2010 flags for protection by changing the settings in the Trust Center.

Working with the Trust Center

You use the Trust Center to set up your preferences for the way your files are opened, shared, and protected. You can create lists of trusted publishers, documents, and locations that don't have to be authenticated each time you receive a document from them.

You'll find the Trust Center by clicking the File tab and clicking Options. At the bottom of the category list, click Trust Center and then click Trust Center Settings. The Active X tab opens by default so that you can review those settings. The following table explains each of the categories in the Trust Center and explains how you can use those options to safeguard your files.

Word 2010 Trust Center

Category	Description
Trusted Publishers	Enables you to create a list of publishers you trust so that any content you receive from the publisher is opened freely without restriction.
Trusted Locations	Gives you the ability to create a list of trustworthy locations—for example, share folders and SharePoint Workspaces.
Trusted Documents	Creates a list of documents you have specified as trusted. After a document is marked as trusted, macros and all content is enabled automatically.
Add-Ins	Enables you to specify whether any application add-ins must be signed by a trusted publisher.
Active X Settings	Lets you choose whether ActiveX controls will be allowed to play in regular mode or in safe mode. You also set the level of restriction for the running of the controls.
Macro Settings	Sets whether macros are automatically disabled or enabled.
Protected View	Enables you to choose the situations in which Protected View is used.
Message Bar	Lets you show or hide the Message Bar.
File Block Settings	Gives you the ability to choose whether specific file types are blocked from being open or saved.
Privacy Options	Lets you set privacy options for the current file.

Changing File Validation

You can tell Word 2010 which file types you want to validate before opening the files. This controls when Protected View is used to safeguard files that you are opening. You can choose that files be checked when you open a file, save a file, or both. The following table introduces the different settings you can choose for file validation.

Set File Types

1. Click the File tab and click Options to display the Word Options dialog box.

2. Click Trust Center.

3. Click the Trust Center Settings button.

4. Click the File Block Settings category.

5. Click to clear the check mark in any file type you don't want to check.

6. Click to add a check mark in the Open and Save columns for those file types you do want to check.

7. Click OK.

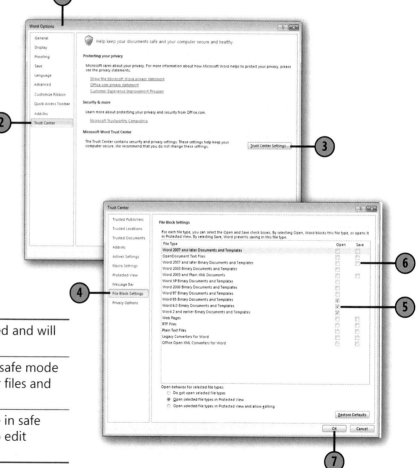

File Block Behaviors

Setting	Description
Do Not Open Selected File Types	The selected files are blocked and will not be opened.
Open Selected File Types In Protected View	Opens the selected file in a safe mode that is protected from other files and processes.
Open Selected File Types In Protected View And Allow Editing	Opens the selected file type in safe mode but allows the user to edit normally.

Choosing What's Displayed in Protected View

The Protected View message bar appears when you have tried to open a file that has either been blocked or has been determined to be in a file format flagged for blocking. If you want to see the contents of the file or know the person or company who sent it, you can open the file in Protected View. Protected View is a safe mode that enables you to view the file without it potentially affecting your other files. When you know the file is okay, you can click Enable Editing to open the file normally.

Word 2010 enables you to choose when Protected View is used for your files. You'll find the settings for Protected View in the Protected View category in the Trust Center.

Set Protected View Settings

1. Click the File tab and click Options to display the Word Options dialog box.

2. Click Trust Center and click Trust Center Settings.

3. Select Protected View.

4. Click to remove the check mark of any setting you do not want to keep.

5. Click OK.

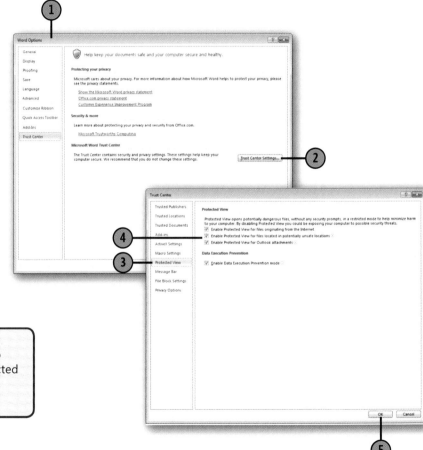

Tip

You can modify the settings at any time. If you later want to restore a protection you removed, simply display the Protected View category again and click the check mark to return the check.

Password Protecting a File

Office 2010, like its predecessors, makes it easy for you add passwords to your Word, Excel, and PowerPoint files. Now in Office 2010, you can add encryption to your password to ensure that your file is as secure as possible.

Add a Password

1. Click the File tab.

2. In the Info tab, click Protect Document in the Permissions area.

3. Click Encrypt with a Password.

4. Enter a password and click OK.

 Tip

You can also set the password during the Save As process by clicking (in the Save As dialog box) the Tools arrow, choosing General Options, and entering the password required to open the file. If you plan to share the file with others, you can enter a separate password that you share with co-authors to enable modification and file sharing.

Caution

Note that when you set an encrypted password for your Word file, the password cannot be recovered if you forget the password later. For this reason, you should keep a copy of your passwords in a safe place you can access easily.

Limiting File Changes

Not only do you need to make sure that the files you open are safe, but you also need to be able to protect the files you create so that people can change only what you want them to change in the file. You can set protection levels on individual files that make it possible for you to limit editing in a document, for example, or protect sections or the structure of a worksheet, so that others' ability to change the content of the file is limited.

Set File Permissions

1. Click the File tab.

2. In the Info tab, click Protect Document.

3. Click Restrict Editing to control the types of editing that can be done in the file.

(continued on next page)

Tip

Formatting restrictions limit users to changing styles used in the document, and editing restrictions enable you to specify whether you want users to view the file as read-only, or if you will allow them to enter tracked changes, comments, or complete forms.

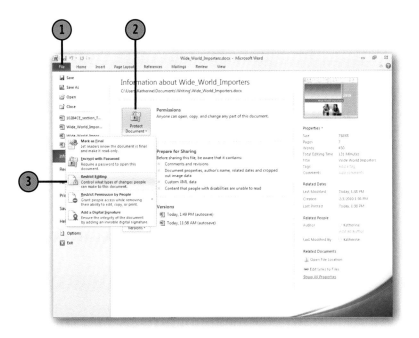

Set File Permissions *(continued)*

(4) Click the Allow Only This Type Of Editing In The Document check box.

(5) Click the type of change you want to allow.

(6) Indicate who these changes apply to.

(7) Click Yes, Start Enforcing Protection.

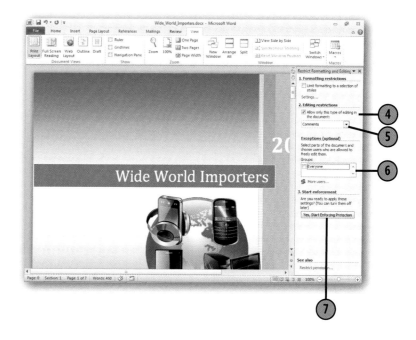

Tip

You can also limit the access others have to your files by restricting the permissions they have based on their role. The Restrict Permission By People option in the Protect Document settings in the Info tab (in Backstage view) enable you to choose the group of people who you want to give access to your document.

Tip

Word gives you the option of adding a digital signature to your document to verify a document's integrity. The digital signature feature in each of these applications requires a signature service from a third-party vendor. You can begin the process by clicking Add A Digital Signature in the Protect Document selection of the Info tab, and a prompt will offer you the option of finding a signature service on Office Marketplace. Note that Protect Document is not available if you are using Compatibility Mode—you must first save the document as a Word 2010 file before Protect Document becomes available.

Recovering Unsaved Versions

Have you ever made great changes to a document and then accidentally closed the file without saving? One of the great new safety-net features in Word 2010 is your file is saved for you in case you forget. Because the program stores your unsaved files automatically, you can return to a previous version if you need to find information you accidentally deleted or items you revised in error.

Recover Unsaved Files

1. Click the File tab.

2. Click Manage Versions.

3. Click Recover Unsaved Versions.

4. Select the file you want and click Open.

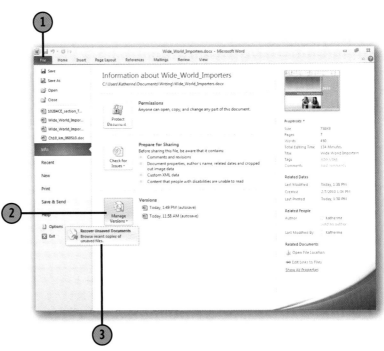

Index

Symbols

A

B

C

H

I

X

XML Word Document format, 158

Z

Zoom control, 8, 12, 33, 104, 179
Zoom tool, 25

About the Author

Katherine Murray is the author or co-author of 40+ computer books, including *First Look Microsoft® Office 2010, Microsoft® Word 2003 Inside Out*, and *First Look 2007 Microsoft® Office System*. She is also a columnist on the Microsoft® Office Community site at Microsoft.com.

What do you think of this book?

We want to hear from you!

To participate in a brief online survey, please visit:

microsoft.com/learning/booksurvey

Tell us how well this book meets your needs—what works effectively, and what we can do better.
Your feedback will help us continually improve our books and learning resources for you.

Thank you in advance for your input!

Stay in touch!

To subscribe to the *Microsoft Press® Book Connection Newsletter*—for news on upcoming books, events, and special offers—please visit:

microsoft.com/learning/books/newsletter